LISTEN TO MY HEART

EDITOR: Amy Bee
TRANSLATIONS: Anna Berglund
COVER PHOTO: Mattias Edwall
COVER DESIGN: Midnight Marauder
LAYOUT: Arkadii Pankevich

Additional photo credits appear in the back of the book.

LIBRARY OF CONGRESS CONTROL NUMBER: 2022946041
LC record available at https://lccn.loc.gov/2022946041

ISBNs: 9781948221245 (hardbound), 9781948221238 (limited edition hardbound w/CD), 9781948221252 (ebook)

1984 Publishing logo is © and ™ of 1984 Publishing, LLC

Printed and bound in PRC.

1984 PUBLISHING
Cleveland, Ohio / USA
1984Publishing.com
info@1984publishing.com

FIRST EDITION
9 8 7 6 5 4 3 2 1

MARIE FREDRIKSSON

LISTEN TO MY HEART

— LIFE, LOVE & ROXETTE —

HELENA VON ZWEIGBERGK

CONTENTS

Chapters

FOREWORD

For thirty years I have spent time in rooms with creative, inspiring people — people with voice and vision, beauty and heart. But I have never met someone quite like Marie.

Marie Fredriksson was one of the most full-fledged artists I've ever had the pleasure of knowing. She radiated creativity in her thoughts, ideas, execution, and her very presence in the room. Her artistry flowed (and continues to flow) straight from her heart and into yours, as anyone fortunate enough to have seen her perform can attest.

I am one of those fortunate people. My friendship with Marie started in the earliest days of my career. She trusted me to help realize her 1992 solo LP *The Constant Journey* into a visual album. Then, and in every project since, I have admired Marie's courage. The courage to allow the open, honest, vulnerable person within to shine through her art.

Marie was my first true break in the industry, and I'll always be grateful for that — not only because of the projects that followed, but because of the integrity, focus, and creative generosity that she taught me. A generosity she carried throughout the entire time I knew her, in every project we ever embarked on together. She was always inspiring, always great fun to be with.

Creative work was a way of life for Marie. No matter what obstacle, adversity, or strange surprise life threw at her, Marie never stopped giving us the gift of her expression — her voice, her words, and her beautiful paintings. This book is but one testament to the boundless creativity she exuded throughout her life.

If I could say one thing to her, I would tell her: *The world is a less interesting and creative place without you, my dear friend. Our lives are less fun, less full of possibility without you. You gave us an unending well of beauty and memories that I will always treasure. Your voice stays with us, forever.*

Marie Fredriksson was liquid gold. She was the light in our lives. She gifted us with moments we will never forget. I am so proud to have known and worked with her. A true artist in every aspect, with a damn good singing voice.

Jonas Åkerlund
JonasÅkerlund.com
Fall 2022

Jonas Åkerlund and Marie Fredriksson on the music video set of Roxette's "Wish I Could Fly," 1998.

PROLOGUE

There is an almost mythical quality to the expression in Marie Fredriksson's eyes.

I noticed it in the fall of 2013 when we first met to discuss this book. She radiated enigmatic wisdom, like she'd lived a life not easily articulated, her time on earth filled with extraordinary experiences that transcended words. Her eyes spoke of long journeys of the heart and mind, through the realms of darkness and light, and a fierce, hard-earned knowledge gained from traveling the world.

When Marie locked eyes with me, I immediately realized the serious nature behind her request. The act of telling her story, putting it together, finding meaning within it, and sharing it with others would be an accomplishment. One of the effects of her brain tumor had been memory loss, yet glimpses of her past were returning to her piece by piece, and more than ever, it felt like it was time to reconstruct her own story.

"I want people to know," she said with great determination. "I want people to know what it's like to go through what I've been through."

We were at the family villa in Djursholm. Here Marie lived with her husband Micke [Bolyos], their two children Josefin and Oscar, and the cat, Sessan. We sat on a cream-colored sofa within the beautiful house. White roses bloomed in a crystal vase. Several antiques decorated the living space, including a large, shiny black piano. An eye-catching painting by Einar Jolin held sway over the room. Like many of the other villas in the area, the Bolyos' villa exemplified the beauty, taste, and status afforded to those who had the finances to fulfill such ambitions.

Of course, I wanted to help Marie share her story.

During the time we spent together, from the autumn of 2013 to the summer of 2015, much happened in Marie's life.

Life had been busy and stressful, even though she tried to maintain a sense of peace. She went on her first solo tour since the cancer diagnosis in the fall of 2002. She released the album *Now!* (*Nu!*) together with Micke. She recorded some new songs with Roxette, and the band embarked on a world tour starting in Russia before moving on to Australia and Europe.

Spend any amount of time with Marie, and it's clear she's a fighter with an iron will. She may occasionally need assistance to move from one room to another, yet also travels the world performing nightly in audience-filled arenas.

"What else am I supposed to do," she says, "just lie down and die? I decided early on that I wouldn't do that. To never give up like that."

And then she adds, "And there sure as hell is nothing wrong with my voice!"

During the last two years, we've been meeting in Marie's home. She lives close to the coastal inlet of Stora Värtan in Djursholm — Stockholm's most exclusive suburb, with villas worth several million hidden behind fortified walls and fences. The house is her home and fortress. Some leg pain from radiation treatment has been flaring up, so Marie never goes anywhere alone and barely even visits her garden without company. She's afraid she might fall, so she needs someone to hold on to.

We sit at the family's kitchen table most of the time, drinking coffee and eating pastries. Sometimes when I'm waiting outside of the gate to be let in, I'll notice one of her fans has placed a bouquet in the door handle.

"Oh, the fans," Marie says as I enter with the flowers and accompanying letters. "The fans are so amazing."

Marie's fans are persistent and loving. When Marie had solo concerts during the winter of 2014, travelers came from worldwide to attend shows throughout Sweden. Fans flew in from Argentina, Denmark, Holland, and Germany for a chance to see and hear Marie.

We relax by the kitchen table, allowing space for long-buried words and memories to slowly make their way back up to the surface.

"Oh, my memory," she often says when the conversation comes to a halt.

It's often names that she gets stuck on, or places. But sometimes she's quick, like when I mentioned what an iconic singer and performer she was, and she quickly retorted back, "Is!"

Or when I said how solid her family had been through all the hardship, she answered with the speed of light, "We *are* a solid family."

And another time, when Marie shared painful memories from an intense period of her illness, and I said, "I understand," she immediately replied, "No, you don't. It's impossible without having been there."

It is perhaps difficult to fully comprehend the nightmare of living with a brain tumor, but Marie describes it in a way that imparts a harrowing idea of what it's like.

Marie often talks about herself as a "typical Gemini." For those who know astrology, like her older sister Ulla-Britt, she is a "Double-Twin," a person with strong contrasts in her mind. And the description is strikingly accurate. On the one hand, Marie is a wise, collected, and calm person. And on the other hand, a volatile personality where emotions emerge as suddenly as the weather changes, lightness and darkness.

Marie willingly attests to the darkness. She tells me, "You cannot fathom how dreadful it is. Such grief. Such an immense sadness."

Tears roll down her cheeks, and they're wiped away with a quick stroke of her hand. "But it's getting better. It's getting better all the time. And you have to laugh, too. You must never forget that — to laugh. That's so important."

Marie is quite particular about this being her book, her story. The aim has never been to write a biography where every fact of Marie's life is included and placed in chronological order. This is more a book of emotional memories. What is included is everything that mattered and was essential for Marie to discuss. As she conveyed, "It should be honest. I just want to say it as it is. No fuss. Just as straightforward as possible."

I've spoken to several people close to Marie, and there seems to be a consensus between them. Many mention Marie's big heart. "A big heart in a small body" is how her friend Efva Attling sums her up.

"I've always thought of her as the most energetic member of the band," says Lotta Skoog, a longtime friend of Marie who lives with Pelle Alsing, the drummer in both Roxette and Marie's solo band. "Before Marie got sick, she was always the one keeping the highest pace. In fact, she's probably still the one with the most energy if you take her illness into account. That Marie has the strength and the drive to continue in the way that she has — it's absolutely fantastic."

"She is probably the most generous and brave person that I've ever met," asserts Marika Erlandsson, a friend present during the most difficult part of Marie's illness and lives with Clarence Öfwerman, Roxette's producer and pianist from the very beginning.

Marika clarifies a trait of Marie's that I've marveled at myself during my time with her. She explains, "Even in her darkest moments, she has never displayed any tendency toward envy or bitterness. She never lost her ability to be happy for others. In that regard, she is quite unique."

"Apart from being a good friend, she has been a role model for me since the mid eighties," says Åsa Gessle [Roxette member Per's wife]. "We hung out and traveled together even before Roxette. Per, Marie, and [producer] Lasse Lindbom, for example, had a side project called the Exciting Cheeses, and then I walked around with a hat for donations. We've had so much fun together. I have seen up close how Marie has progressed with enormous will and perseverance. She comes from a simple upbringing and was very shy in the beginning. But with her fantastic singing voice and determination, she turned into an artist who has touched people around the world. She has always believed in her strength and managed to achieve something unparalleled. In that way, she has always been a source of inspiration for me."

And that energy is mentioned more than once. Director Jonas Åkerlund, who made several of Roxette's music videos as well as the documentary *The Constant Journey* about Marie, adds, "She had such amazing energy. Both at work and privately. She could be such a rock star, drinking beer and hanging out at the bar after work. We've had so much fun together. But she's also very creative and puts everything into her work. I have met a lot of superstars, but both Per and her stand out from the crowd as especially down-to-earth and humble. I think it's because they're basically country bumpkins, both of them."

When it comes to describing Marie musically, it tends to sound like this:

"She is a force of nature," explains Thomas Johansson, Live Nation's Chairman of the Board and a friend and business partner for many years. "She really knows how to convey an emotion. It's something in her very essence. She has such capacity in her voice, despite her petite size. She's also part of that group of singers who know how to write lyrics. Elton John, Bruce Springsteen, Rod Stewart, Van Morrison, and Marie are all artists that know how to do that. They're able to tell a story through their music and do so in an authentic way. I don't really know how they do it; maybe they just know how to place the words correctly. If I was allowed to redo everything I have done, I would only be looking for voices like that."

"Marie has a fantastic timing and improvisational ability and a completely unique voice," says Pelle Alsing.

"She is the best singer in Sweden," says Clarence Öfwerman. "It's her and [jazz singer] Monica Zetterlund. She is so vulnerable and gives it everything that she's got. No wonder the entire world loves it. She has that extra something that no one else has."

It's precisely that vulnerability that resonates with people. Marie can sing lyrics that would make someone else sound naive or flat and make them feel completely authentic. Marie makes a simple lyric explode with aspiration. Maybe it's her courage that transforms lyrics from banal to beautiful, her ability to reveal herself, and her audacity to give from the heart without being ironic or smart. "She is very intuitive and makes her material come to life," says Kjell Andersson, who was at the record company EMI where Marie became famous. "She has credibility and is able to reach those who listen. I do not know what it is. She's very open and receptive, from me to you. There's some sort of childlike innocence about it that really hits people in the heart. She also has a clearly visible passion for singing that people are drawn to."

Many people assisted with this book and allowed me to engage in long conversations with them to help Marie reconnect the puzzle pieces of her past. I would like to extend a warm thank you to these individuals: her best friend Pähr Larsson, Marika Erlandsson, Clarence Öfwerman, Anders Herrlin, Per Gessle, Åsa Gessle, Marie Dimberg, Christoffer Lundquist, Lasse Lindbom, Niklas Strömstedt, Efva Attling, Pelle Alsing, Lotta Skoog, Åsa Elmgren, Stefan Dernbrant, Martin Sternhufvud, Ika Nord, Thomas Johansson, Kjell Andersson, and Jonas Åkerlund. Thanks to Marie's original family: Tina Pettersson, Gertie and Sven-Arne Fredriksson, Ulla-Britt Fredriksson, Tony Fredriksson. Thanks to childhood friends Kerstin Junér, Bitte Henrysson, and Boel Andersson. And above all, a thank you to Marie's husband, Mikael Bolyos. He has been there throughout Marie's illness and has not only been a great support for her but an invaluable witness to her memory.

Helena von Zweigbergk
Summer 2015

CHAPTER 1

"It isn't until now that I'm able to use the words *brain tumor*."

Marie's own story about her illness.

───────────

It was September 11, 2002 when all hell broke loose.

Τhe next day, I was supposed to travel to Antwerp, Belgium, where Per Gessle and I were to hold a press conference announcing that Roxette was going on tour with a series of concerts called Night of the Proms, a Belgian phenomenon. I planned to take an early flight on September 12. Per wanted to leave on the eleventh, as he hated getting up early and wanted to sleep in. I didn't want to fly on the anniversary of the terrorist attack on the World Trade Center in New York and thought it was safer to take an early flight the next day.

On the morning of the eleventh, Micke read me an article about the anniversary and a Swedish man who worked in the building. The awful part was that he'd disappeared in the rubble of the collapsed building, and his relatives never found out what had happened to him.

Micke and I discussed the man's fate. How he probably woke up to a typical day, unaware of what awaited him a few hours later. We agreed how nice it is not to know what the future holds. That ignorance of one's future destiny is a kind of blessing. Coincidentally, we didn't realize that a few hours later, on that same day, our entire world would be turned upside down.

After the morning coffee, Micke and I went on our usual morning run. Toward the end, Micke wanted to race, and I outran him.

I was so fast back then.

When we got home, I wasn't feeling that well. I was tired and nauseous and felt like I needed to rest. I didn't have that much time, as I needed to pack for the upcoming flight. But I had to lie down for a bit. All of a sudden, I couldn't see out of one of my eyes. My nausea increased, and I went into the bathroom to vomit. Inside the bathroom, I collapsed. It was terribly frightening. And then, darkness.

I'd gone into an epileptic seizure, which caused my entire body to shake, and I hit my head so hard against the stone floor that I cracked my skull. Of course, I didn't know this then. All I remember was hearing Micke's voice from a distance shouting, "Marie! What happened?" before it turned dark again. I awoke briefly in an ambulance. My vision was blurry, and I heard the sound of sirens. And then I blacked out yet again. When I woke up, Micke and his mother, Berit, were sitting by my bedside.

"What am I doing here?" I asked. "What happened?"

A kindly doctor came into the room and gently asked me if I had plans to go on tour soon. "Yes, of course," I replied. He told me in a calm and friendly voice that I'd probably need to cancel the tour.

Slowly it dawned on me that I was in a hospital and had fallen. But it didn't occur to me that the collapse was due to a brain tumor. I thought it was strange that my vision had been blurry, but otherwise, I thought I'd had an accident. The doctor eventually returned with X-rays and told me they'd found a mass in my brain.

I was completely shocked.

"Am I going to die from it?" I asked. The doctor said no, not from *that* tumor, because it could be operated on and radiated away. That was all I could process at the time: I had a tumor, but it could be removed. I wasn't going to die.

He kept talking, but I couldn't follow the details. Perhaps I didn't want to understand what he was telling me, that the tumor would come back, and it might not be possible to remove it. Micke understood, but I didn't.

None of us wanted any horrible predictions about how small my chances were. We wanted to fight and keep our hopes up as long as possible. Another doctor, an acquaintance of ours, took care of my skull injury. Since he knew us, the hospital staff thought he might as well be the one to tell us the whole truth. He informed Micke that I had one year left to live. Micke turned completely white and almost fainted, and the doctor quickly added that I might live for two years.

Or maybe even three.

That was the most comforting thing he could say. At best, I could live for another three years.

Micke felt he had to hide from me how bad it was. I was so hopeful and focused on it all working out. *That was what the doctor had said*, I was thinking, and that soon everything would be back to normal.

It was the beginning of quite a miserable period for Micke. He started thinking about how to prepare the kids for their mother's death. Josefin was nine years old then, and Oscar five. The future was like an approaching monstrosity, and Micke couldn't do anything to hold it back. He had to wait for what seemed like an inevitability with his hands tied behind his back. He was terrified to watch me fade away before his eyes, unable to do anything.

To be so completely powerless.

Poor, poor Micke. How was he supposed to shatter my hope and tell me that I would probably die?

Micke's inability to be honest with me felt to him as if life had put a wedge between us. We'd always talked openly about everything. Always. Neither of us ever turned away from the other, and we rarely had conflicts. Nothing had ever happened that we couldn't work through. And now, suddenly, we were in the middle of a life-and-death situation that Micke couldn't candidly speak to me about. He thought I should live with hope. He wanted to keep my spirits high and encourage me, even though he was living a completely different truth.

A truth we couldn't talk our way out of.

I'd set my mind on making it, but deep down I thought there was a chance it might not end well. When I was about to fall asleep in the evenings during that initial shocking period, thoughts like that crept in, and I never wanted to tell Micke about them. Or the kids. The children sometimes asked me if I was going to die. I'd reply that I wasn't, and didn't have time for that. But deep down, in the middle of the night, I thought it might indeed happen.

I wanted to talk about how everything would be fine and didn't want to outwardly show otherwise. In that way, both Micke and I had similar thoughts, yet were still alone in the situation.

―――

I had a crack in my skull from the fall and a balance disorder, so I got a wheelchair to take home from the hospital. Oscar thought it was the best toy in the world. Oh, how he would ride around in that thing, being all like — *woo-hoo*!

When I later sat around the house without hair and was quite sad, Oscar would suddenly come in pretending to be Batman and get me laughing. Thank goodness we had such moments.

Lots of flowers were sent to our home, which was lovely. I received a fantastic bouquet from ABBA's Anni-Frid Lyngstad, which made me happy. Micke sometimes thought it was sad with all the flowers around. They symbolized grief and tragedy, and our home sometimes resembled a cemetery to him. But he also thought it was kind of people to show us that they were thinking about us.

It was far worse with the media. The night after I rode to the hospital in the ambulance, *The Express* (*Expressen*) called and woke my siblings in Skåne for comments before we'd even had time to inform them of the situation. They were pretty scared and shocked. And the press terrorized them. "Did they know anything new?" "Had they heard anything?"

I don't know how the newspapers found out so quickly. They may have monitored our address and learned from the emergency center that an ambulance had been called. Or they were tipped off by someone at the hospital.

Our nanny, Inger, told us that the first night in the hospital, journalists called on our intercom at home in Djursholm until three o'clock in the morning. The journalists followed Inger when she left and picked up the children from school. Both she and the children were terrified. We eventually hired three security guards who worked in shifts to protect us. In addition, we kept the home dark to avoid the paparazzi's attempts to get photos of the family inside the house.

There was one time when Micke couldn't leave with the car. He had to step out and ask them if it was necessary for them to block the road. One journalist felt a bit of shame and replied that his newspaper had ordered him to stand there. We don't know if the other journalists felt embarrassed, but we were under siege there for a while.

Roxette's and my manager, Marie Dimberg, contacted my siblings to tell them they didn't need to answer any questions and could hang up when the media called. My siblings are kind souls who weren't used to being rude to people and felt compelled to help as best they could.

The press wouldn't stop calling Marie [Dimberg]. As soon as she received updates from any of us about my condition, the newspapers called immediately afterward. Someone at the hospital was leaking information. The press would somehow get medical updates at about the same time as we did, and then would chase after Marie to confirm or deny. She spoke to the press service and the security department at Karolinska Hospital to stop the leaks.

The press heard almost immediately that I had a brain tumor, and were relentless with everyone in our circle to obtain confirmation. It made us feel obligated to tell our story. Marie therefore sent out a short press release but chose Sunday night, as there was an election happening, so the newspapers wouldn't be able to run it as a lead story. One newspaper did so anyway.

The surgeons removed the tumor, and I had a so-called Gamma Knife surgery the following year. They attached a metal crown with a y-axis and an x-axis to my head. The radiation needed to hit precisely the right place in the brain — millimeter precision. They screwed the crown into my skull while I was awake. I received ointment as an anesthetic, one used by dentists. I still felt blood and tears running down my head. It was probably the worst of all my treatments. It was so nasty. Like a crown of thorns! Micke thought he would vomit when he saw it.

There were some absurd moments in the middle of it all. Like after the Gamma Knife surgery, a doctor we hadn't met entered the room and wanted to tell me about his garage band and his guitar. We were waiting to hear the result of a challenging radiation treatment, with the crown still screwed into my head, while this doctor expected me to be interested in his garage band. I don't think he even worked in the neurology department.

What are some people thinking?

As a public figure in the hospital, many people want to come in, take a look, and make contact. A nurse told me about her abusive husband and how she wanted to divorce him but lacked the $16,000 (150000 SEK) to get an apartment. Micke and I got the feeling that she was fishing for money. We went through several incidents like that.

It was a time of unbearable waiting — month after month of living with overwhelming anxiety over how my condition might develop. There were evenings when the children were watching television, and Micke and I sat across from each other in the kitchen, eating dinner in silence with tears rolling down our cheeks and into our soup bowls. Whenever one of the children came in, we'd wipe away the tears and try to pull ourselves together.

We changed as parents. It was inevitable. We tried not to be so absorbed by sadness and worry, but it was omnipresent. It consumed us. We weren't as focused on the children as before. I had mentally shut out the shock of what had happened, and Micke was constantly worried. Our distraction affected them. And when we were sad like that, Micke and I wanted to escape from reality. We often drank too much wine in the evenings and lived as if every day could be the last.

Even though the stress made it difficult to be fully available to the children, our anxiety mainly revolved around them. I thought all the time, *the kids, the kids. What if I die now? A mother can't die. I have to take care of the kids! And Micke!* Pressure churned inside of me. *Is this when I'm gonna die? Is this when I'm gonna die?*

But then came the divine power. *I can't die now!* I've had strong faith ever since I was little. I keep it private, but it's within me. When I was a child, I loved singing in the church choir. I felt strong trust and comfort there. The power of my faith carried me through many difficult times.

Still, even with faith, life was in limbo. We tried to live as we used to, even though it was often impossible. We got our cat, Sessan, so the children had something else to think about. And we tried to keep the traditions we had with the children alive, even though we were mostly in the hospital.

We used to have a treasure hunt with them every Friday. The treasure was a bag of sweets they had to look for. We would easily spend half a Friday making elaborate plans on how to go about it. After I became ill, we tried to recreate the hunt in the hallway at Karolinska Hospital. We only did it once. Something had changed. It felt a bit over the top to try and pretend like everything was normal.

I can't talk about the inadequacy I've felt as a mother due to my brain tumor without starting to cry. Before I got sick, I was a strong person who kept things in order. Not being able to be the kind of parent that you want to be is perhaps the worst thing about the disease.

Some people who've experienced similar difficulties say that they didn't know how good they had it before being affected. But we knew. We often said to each other how fortunate we were. When I see the children's school photos taken just before I got sick, it strikes me. We were so incredibly happy together. We had everything — love, success, health.

I thought it was fortunate that the children were too small to understand. Yes, Josefin probably understood, but Oscar wasn't sure what had happened. They spent a lot of time with Inger during the most critical times while I was in and out of different hospitals.

Micke prayed for the children to grow a few years older before I died. He told me this in retrospect. He wanted them to have time to get a clear picture of their mother, a chance to remember me properly. He knew it was a lot to ask.

The radiation made me lose my hair. During Christmas, more and more tufts came off my scalp. Micke was afraid that it would be the last Christmas we would experience together. And it could have been.

I'd been so incredibly fortunate.

In January, six months after discovering the tumor, Roxette was awarded a medal by the King of Sweden.

Micke figured they probably thought I would die soon and felt rushed. He was probably right. Still, I was flattered and happy about the recognition. At the same time, it was difficult. It required me to appear in public, and I hadn't been around the public since I became ill. And I was pretty much bald. Marie and I went out looking for a hat for me and found one in a leopard pattern.

Late on the evening before the medal ceremony, then *Express* reporter Niclas Rislund rang Marie's door. He said he'd received information that my cancer had metastasized and spread to my breasts and the rest of my body. Marie said she wouldn't comment on rumors about my health; she'd rather go back to bed and sleep. He persisted and demanded Marie call me to get confirmation. Marie asked him to show consideration and leave me alone. He said he'd write his piece either way, so she might as well do what he said.

Marie got very angry. They shouted at each other. He claimed that she had specific responsibilities as the spokesperson of a public figure. Marie shouted back that she had no obligation whatsoever to inform him and *The Express* about the current state of my illness and slammed her door on him. The next morning Marie called and asked if we had read *The Express*.

We hadn't.

"Then don't," she said. "Avoid it if you can."

But how could we avoid *The Express*? Its headline was displayed all over town, declaring that the cancer had spread. The whole article was fueled by the perception that I didn't have much time left to live.

It wasn't true that I had breast cancer or that the cancer metastasized, and Marie Dimberg went out with a press statement and denied it. *The Express'* then editor-in-chief referred to reliable sources at Karolinska Hospital. As a family, we took it quite hard. And I was still expected to go and receive a medal from the king that same day.

I can't convey how surreal it was to read a story like that. To be incorrectly and salaciously sentenced to death in front of everyone. To also feel unsafe in a hospital, knowing people were lurking around and trying to gain something from your misfortune. For some, your sorrow was nearly a treat for them to enjoy.

I was so nervous when I received the medal that I accidentally held it upside down. It felt like everyone was staring and wanted to see how sick I looked. They wanted to gawk at the woman that they'd read about, the one who was riddled with cancer throughout her body. The one who was dying. That turned out to be a terrible day.

To deal with *The Express'* lies in the middle of it all was the last thing we needed. On their initiative, the Chancellor of Justice even reported the hospital Karolinska. The doctor who'd operated on me called us in surprise, saying five policemen had come to the hospital and searched his office. It was unpleasant for him, but he was as interested as we were in finding the leak. Violating the confidentiality law is a serious crime resulting in up to three years in prison.

Many people were upset about *The Express'* handling of us. The TV show *Mediamagasinet* called it one of the most scandalous infractions in modern press. We were so offended and hurt that we looked into the possibility of suing *The Express*. In addition, we wanted to show the children that they weren't allowed to lie and make up stories about us.

We decided to contact a well-known lawyer with experience in media issues. In retrospect, one would think he would've advised us against it straight away. We thought journalists weren't allowed to lie about someone having a fatal diagnosis, quite simply, and that the lies were enough to file a lawsuit. Unfortunately, it wasn't legally enough to say that someone had behaved immorally or proved to be insensitive to other people's suffering.

The lawyer nevertheless tried to find a helpful paragraph for us. He found a legal precedent where someone had used a picture of two people having sexual intercourse and replaced their faces with those of some famous people. The case was about slander and putting someone in a bad light. He thought that this was how we were going to beat *The Express*.

Our lawyer for this situation was an odd acquaintance to make. One of the first things he said during our contact was that his daughter, a big Roxette fan, was turning forty soon, and he'd asked one of the evening papers to make a mock-up headline that stated she was the third member of Roxette. He wondered if Per and I could sign it. An unbecoming first request from our lawyer, who was supposed to help us through the worst period of our life. As if it was some sort of game.

Our only chance to beat *The Express*, according to the lawyer, was to claim that *The Express'* lies had put me in a bad light. He wanted Micke to tell the court that he'd thought I'd lied to him when he saw the headlines. He was supposed to act like a hurt husband who thought his wife hadn't told him the truth about her illness.

Micke told him that he wouldn't say it because it seemed absurd for him to lie like that. So even though we had already spent hundreds of thousands trying to sue *The Express*, we stopped. It would take at least five years of our time, and we'd have to go over everything again and again.

The whole *Express* scandal was a costly and unpleasant experience for us. We were a shocked and vulnerable family who didn't deserve to be used to sell newspapers. We consider *The Express'* editor as someone who has caused our family great harm, and he's never apologized for it.

It was true that there was uncertainty about whether I'd survive, but no goddamned cancer was spreading through my body. The microscopic streak of hope we had was the only thing that made us function. Maybe that was why *The Express'* lies were so unbearable. The lie portrayed me as sicker than I was and thus extinguished any hope in the eyes of the world around me.

It hurt so terribly.

━━━━━━━

I tried my best to be creative during this period. Shortly after the first operation, Micke and I made the album *The Change*. The record was a culmination of the work we'd started before I got sick. We'd already recorded a cover song called "The Good Life" together. Now the album was about making the most out of the good things in life amid our tragedy.

We worked with the recording engineer Lennart Östlund, who was so cool. We didn't have to dwell on the disease all the time, even though Micke still had to call doctors and check my vocal keynotes. Working on this record was a free zone. I still think it's one of the best projects we've done together. The lyrics quite naturally came to be about the joy of being alive. In the darkest darkness, we created a bright record. This is one of the darker texts on it, but it describes how I felt then:

> *Suddenly the change was here*
> *Cold as ice and full of fear*
> *There was nothing I could do*
> *I saw slow-motion pictures of me and you*
>
> *Far away, I heard you cry*
> *My table roses slowly died*
> *Suddenly the change was here*
> *I took your hands; you dried my tears*
> *The night turned into black and blue*
> *Still, we wondered why me and you*
> *After all, we're still here*
> *I held your hand; I felt no fear*
>
> *Memories will fade away*
> *Sun will shine on a new clear day*
> *New red roses in my hand*
> *Maybe someday we will understand*
> *Maybe one day we will understand*

The lyrics capture things the way they were: despair, love, confusion, and at the same time, an intense longing for hope and a need to take in every piece of light available.

No matter how sick I've been, I've always tried to keep the creative side of myself. For Micke, taking care of me became a full-time job. He drove me back and forth to the hospital and helped me remember what they said about medications and treatments.

News of my illness spread around the world. My fans sent a list of names and told me they'd started a prayer chain for me, praying for me to survive. I framed that letter, and it's one of my dearest possessions. It meant a lot to me.

Many also contacted us with suggestions for alternative treatments. "Deposit $20,000 into this account and swallow this sand." Outrageous tips like that. An Egyptian doctor at a university in China was one of those who contacted us. Micke asked our cancer doctor Stefan Einhorn what he thought about this individual. Einhorn told us that the doctor had lectured at Karolinska but that he was a fraud.

Dr. Einhorn, to comfort us, told us about his father's cancer. A doctor told his father that he only had one year left to live, but the doctor himself died before Dr. Einhorn's father did. He wanted to illustrate that we never know how much time we have at our disposal. He was trying to give us a different perspective. It was with the best of intentions, but it wasn't overly comforting. We wanted to hear of a solution, that perhaps I could take a pill or a form of treatment and get well. That was just about all that might have given us relief at the time.

We also contacted Vidarkliniken, the anthroposophist [spiritual] hospital. They have clinics that treat cancer. But their kind of care seemed more like a hospice. The patients engaged in art in various forms. The doctor there was quite dreadful. He lectured me, almost as if I was to blame for getting cancer. According to him, since the tumor grew in my body, I was responsible for it being there. I had caused it myself. I totally broke down. I could only handle friendly people, and he was strict and judgmental. He claimed that I'd damaged my immune system by drinking alcohol. I will never forget him and have never felt as bleak as I did then, faced with his heartless diatribe.

In any case, he prescribed some natural extract that we could only pick up in Järna. A taxi had to go and pick it up from time to time. It took three hours and cost us several thousand kronor every time. You're not very assertive in that situation; you simply do as you've been told.

Micke left no stone unturned; he researched everything. His desk was full of different notes we weren't allowed to touch. He contacted a cancer expert in the US and started mailing my X-rays to him. We got an appointment. The hospital was in Houston, Texas. But I decided against it. I didn't have the strength. I wanted peace and quiet and didn't want to travel left and right. It was simply too much.

We asked Dr. Einhorn what he thought about it. He said we could either look for an alternative treatment like Micke was doing or do nothing [and continue with Swedish treatment]. And those two options were equally good. The cancer treatment in Sweden was of such a high standard, he said, that we might as well stay local. So, we decided to trust Swedish cancer care. It was a relief, as everything became calmer after that.

Micke tried to prepare me for dying. It was difficult for him to know what I wanted my funeral to be like, for example, without breaking the defensive walls that I had put up to protect myself from the outside world. He contacted [neurological clinic] Erstagårdskliniken, where we received joint therapy to be able to handle a death in the family. We sat and talked, but I couldn't admit that we were actually speaking about my situation.

He also called a priest from Östra Ljungby, the same priest who had overseen my confirmation rite, our wedding, and our children's baptisms. The priest was very kind and sympathetic. He came to our home to meet us. During the meeting, I mostly cried and didn't understand — or didn't want to understand — what everyone wanted to talk to me about. Micke used various tricks to get me to talk. For example, he told me what kind of funeral he'd like to have and asked me how I'd like mine.

How horrible it is to remember these moments!

───────

It's been over thirteen years, and do you know what? It isn't until now that I'm able to use the words *brain tumor*.

For a long time, I couldn't say it out loud. The shock and grief lasted for several years. It was so hard for me to take in how sick I was, even though it dawned on me more and more. I preferred not to talk about it. It didn't exist if I didn't confess it. The realization that I would die was something I could only admit for a few moments to myself at night.

In front of others, I didn't want acknowledgment of anything having to do with illness and death. I pretended everything was as it should be, although anyone could see it was not. It must've been like living with a big elephant in the room for my family.

I can talk about it now. The grief broke through. Before, it stood still. Now Micke and I can openly discuss the disease. But it took time. It took me so long even to admit I was sick. That is why this book is so meaningful to me. I want others to know what it's been like. Maybe it can give hope or comfort to someone else.

CHAPTER 2

Helsingborg on Wednesday,
February 1, 2014

Back to where it all began.

———————

It's late, and I'm sitting in the restaurant section of Hotel Marina Plaza in Helsingborg waiting for Marie and Micke to come and celebrate the premiere of her first solo tour since she became ill.

We're having a late snack consisting of Toast Skagen and cold white wine. Several are waiting, including Thomas Johansson and Staffan Holm from Live Nation, Kjell Andersson, one of the managers at EMI when Marie first became famous in the eighties, Marie Dimberg, and Marie's friends Pähr Larsson and Christian Bergh.

The atmosphere buzzes with anticipation. Everyone wants to congratulate and hug her. The show was great! So much worry and doubt preceded the tour's premiere. Especially from Marie herself. With her troublesome foot and poor balance, would she be able to make it alone on stage?

The answer was a resounding yes. The feedback from the audience was warm and appreciative. "We love you, Marie!" shouted fans who came from abroad. "We love you!"

Fans sit in another part of the restaurant, waiting to glimpse their beloved idol. They come from Denmark, Holland, Argentina, Spain, and many other countries. Earlier in the evening, I asked some of them why they traveled to Marie's first show to hear her sing in a language they didn't speak. They all answered me in roughly the same way: she connects with them. Even though none of them speak Swedish, they comprehend what she's singing about. It's about emotions. No one can convey feelings as she does, they said.

The international fans know most of Marie's classics: "Faith (Tro)," "There's Still a Scent of Love (Ännu doftar kärlek)," "If You Saw Me Now (Om du såg mig nu)," "The Seventh Wave (Den sjunde vågen)," "After the Storm (Efter stormen)," and "Sparrow-Eye (Sparvöga)." But they also appreciated the songs from the new album *Now!* (*Nu!*), songs like "Come Rest with Me (Kom vila hos mig)" and the self-composed "The Last Waltz of the Summer (Sommarens sista vals)." Now they sit with drinks in front of them, occasionally casting their eyes toward the direction they think Marie might arrive.

It wasn't a given that Marie would embark on this tour. But she was determined to show herself and the outside world that she could return. She felt she had to do it for herself. For the love of the old songs. For the joy of singing the new ones. And to meet her Swedish audience, which often ended up second to Roxette's fans.

Micke was skeptical and thought Marie should save her energy for Roxette's big world tour, which will start at the end of October. Once he realized how important it was for Marie, he gave his full support and offered to play the piano during the tour. The rest of the band are fr Marie feels completely comfortable with. Pelle Alsing from Roxette on drums, Roxette guitarist and co-producer of *Now!* Christoffer Lundquist, nephew and guitarist Jocke Pettersson, and a new acquaintance on bass, Surjo Benigh. Marie often mentions how much she appreciates the musicians she brings on tour. How they support her, encourage her, believe in her, and comfort her when needed.

One of the challenges of the tour has been memorizing the old lyrics. With Marie's neurological injuries, it's been tough. Stanza by stanza, line by line, she attempts to master the lyrics. Only one of her songs has remained intact, and she knew the words right from the start: "There's Still a Scent of Love."

"I'll remember it forever," she said about the song. "Flowers and love — it's impossible to forget things like that!"

We notice a flurry of excitement, and the international fans are applauding. Two hours after the concert's end, Marie arrives, a little tired around the eyes, but a wide, happy smile stretches across her face. She's walking slowly, supported by Micke's arm.

"Are you relieved, happy?" I ask.

"You better believe it!" she says. "It was fantastic. What an audience!"

Marie was late to her premiere party because of the insane amount of hugs and kisses after the concert. Relatives and friends had gathered in the audience, and afterward, it was an ecstatic reunion backstage. It's not too often that Marie is in her old hometown. Sometimes she goes to Östra Ljungby, her childhood village, and visits her oldest sibling, her brother Sven-Arne and his wife, Gertie. They live right next to the house where Marie grew up. Occasionally she visits Rydebäck, where her sister Tina and her family live.

Marie sits down, and shrimp sandwiches arrive at the table. We raise our glasses to the successful premiere. Now they're going to tour around the country for two months. Marie chats about what she could've done differently or a bit better. She's relieved and happy but not one hundred percent satisfied. Such conflicting feelings are often the case during touring, she admits. Singers tend to obsess about their mistakes, no matter how small they are.

Most importantly, Marie's glowing from the overwhelming love she received when the people of her past crowded around her in her dressing room. It was a touching moment, surrounded by the people closest to her as a child.

Marie talks about her childhood in the same way she talks about many things in life, with sharp contrasts. Light, warmth, love. But also darkness, fear, and tragedy.

CHAPTER 3

"I wanted to see it all — the whole world!"

In Marie's words.

I grew up in Östra Ljungby in northwestern Skåne. It's a small town located along the freeway between Åstorp and Örkelljunga, 30 km from Helsingborg.

Not much is there. Well, I remember an incredibly kind hot dog vendor. I never had any money but often got a hot dog anyway. Two grocery stores, a flower shop, a convenience store, and three cafés. The church. The sports field. Often windy and cold. That is a summary of Östra Ljungby.

One of my first memories is when we arrived at our new house there. When I see the brick house today it looks so small. But when I was four years old, it was truly grand. I'll never forget it. It was amazing to come to a house that was our own. And to have a bathroom! The house we lived in before had an outhouse and only cold water. My sister Tina and I jumped up and down on our parents' bed feeling like we would burst with joy. We thought it was so new and nice.

It wasn't that big, as I said. There were three bedrooms all in all. Me and my sister Tina, who was three years older than me, shared a bedroom with our parents. My older sisters Anna-Lisa and Ulla-Britt shared another one, and my big brother Sven-Arne had a whole room to himself.

We were a large family. Everyone had double names — that was quite common back then. I'm christened Gun-Marie and Tina is Inga-Stina. And there's Sven-Arne, Ulla-Britt, and Anna-Lisa. I also had a friend named Eva-Karin. Both Tina and I changed our double names when we got older. But as a child, I was called Gun-Marie, even at school. Or they would say *Gunsan, Majsan,* or *Gun.* It wasn't until later that I decided just to be named Marie.

Sven-Arne, born 1942, Anna-Lisa, born 1945, and Ulla-Britt, born 1947, were all significantly older than Tina and I, who were born in 1955 and 1958. Tina was a 'trailing child,' and when I was born, she was accustomed to being the youngest child, so she wasn't exactly ecstatic about having a little sister. That feeling disappeared over time. We grew up being very close and endeared to each other. The older siblings moved away from home when I was only in elementary school, so Tina and I were the only children in the house for many years.

Before moving to Östra Ljungby, we lived in a small place in Össjö. I was born there on May 30, 1958. My father, Gösta, had a farm, and also ran his father's farm. My grandfather was a widower and very frail. He'd suffered problems for several harvest seasons, including floods. To cope, Gösta reluctantly borrowed money from the bank. And to borrow the funds, two of his siblings had to go in as guarantors. Eventually, it became unsustainable. The siblings were forced to repay the loans, which created discord. Bankruptcy was a painful blow to our family. Sven-Arne remembers when they came to collect the cows, and Ulla-Britt remembers the sound of the auctioneer's gavel hitting the sound block as our home was sold piece by piece. I don't remember anything about it since I was so young.

We had no choice but to rent a drafty, cramped house with only cold water. I spent my first years there. It was often very chilly. When Dad saw how I struggled to cut out paper dolls because my fingers were stiff, he decided we had to find somewhere else to live. And that's how we ended up in Östra Ljungby.

The hope for the future was back. Sven-Arne and Anna-Lisa were old enough to start working and contribute to the household. Dad got a job as a country mailman, and sometimes I got to go on the postal rounds with him. I loved it! We sang together, Father and I, and I always stood in the car, curious to see everything, the whole world. If I wasn't singing, I was talking incessantly. I was called Little Miss Chatterbox, and never sat still. I played outside all day long and got so tan that I looked like a gingerbread man even in the early spring.

I often had a surplus of energy. I'd sing, pestering my father. "What should I do, what should I do?"

He always answered the same thing. "Run a lap around the house."

"I've done that now. What else?"

"Run one more lap."

My father was a fantastic singer. He sang like [Swedish tenor] Jussi Björling. Music was his life. He also played several instruments. He probably would've become an opera singer if he lived under different circumstances. But I don't think he even considered it, doing something that might come across as high-handed to others.

All us sisters sang, too. But my mother, Inez, and Sven-Arne weren't interested in singing. Sven-Arne was mostly shy. We nagged Mother to sing sometimes; it was fun to annoy her that way.

"Come on, Mom. Sing something for us."

"La la la," she said. "There, I sang something."

Music was vital to the whole family. Dad constantly played and sang. We children sang along, and he taught us to dance the hambo and the schottische.

We were often in church. The church had a talented cantor named Bengt Göran Göransson, and we sang in his children's choir. When my sister Ulla-Britt got married to her Danish Jesper in 1970, Tina and I helped him rehearse Beethoven's love song. As you can imagine, there wasn't a dry eye in the house.

I was an early bird and the first in the family to wake. I'd wake Tina by lying in my bed and singing loudly. I referred to it as singing an opera with loud arias. It drove Tina mad.

"Shut up, I want to sleep," she'd shout.

But I couldn't help it. I always wanted to sing. That's still the case. Micke and the children are used to it.

━━━━━━━━

It was difficult for my parents to make ends meet. Sometimes we ate *mjölkasoppa*. It's old bread eaten with warm milk, sprinkled with sugar and cinnamon. I hated it. I can barely say the word now and get nauseated hearing it. We only ate fruit for Christmas, as we couldn't afford it otherwise. When the family came across bananas, we only got to eat half of one. If there was an edge left of the cheese, it wasn't thrown away. We'd take a grater and dip our sandwiches into the cheese gratings.

We didn't have much money, but it was also a different time, and people were more frugal and less wasteful than they are today. Mother and Father sewed children's clothes at home for a clothing company. We packed into the car and drove to Helsingborg to deliver the garments; my father was always irritated at me for kicking the front seat and not sitting still. Dad smoked incessantly in the car, and Tina and I often got motion sickness. But there were also exciting trips, like when we went over to Helsingör to buy less expensive food, and each got an ice cream cone with whipped cream and jam. They tasted delicious!

The children's clothes didn't provide enough money, so my mother started working shifts at the Björnekulla jam factory. Tina and I thought it was a little embarrassing. Most of our friends had their mothers at home. Every other week, she worked in the evenings so she could take care of us in the mornings. But that meant every other week we had to take care of ourselves. Sometimes there was no bread, and sometimes no money.

I was six years old when my mother started working at the factory. I'd lie under the table at home, frightened because I kept hearing noises. It was awful to lie there and be scared. I didn't feel safe and anxiously waited for Dad to come home after the mail round. Once Dad came home, all he wanted was to sleep.

I've always had a hard time being alone. It started in my childhood when I had to fend for myself. Such things leave their mark. Nowadays, I can sometimes appreciate time alone. As long as someone comes home in the evening, it's all right. But if Micke disappeared from my life, I'd have a hard time coping. I grew up in a big family. Having people around was typical. For us, loneliness was an unnatural state.

When my mother was home in the mornings, she made breakfast. And she baked delicious cookies. It's important to remember the positive things, like the days when Father got paid, and we'd get a treat. I loved those days.

We weren't hungry. But we wore hand-me-downs and dreamed of wearing clothes that were new. Sometimes we bought items through the mail-order chain Ellos, which was extra exciting. Mother also got canned goods from the jam factory when they had something wrong with their label or a minor defect. We'd eat those. For Christmas, we bought half a pig. And every Sunday, we ate a proper dinner with meat included. We'd have änglamat, a cake with cookie crumbles, whipped cream, and jam for dessert. It was wonderful to have such a feast.

———

On December 11, 1965, when I was seven years old, a tragedy changed my family's life forever.

Those years, children went to school on Saturdays. I had a small bicycle that I rode to school. It was a slippery and muddy day, snow mixed with rain. When I got to the schoolyard, an older guy came up to me.

"Hey, they're saying that your sister's dead!"

I was shocked. "Don't say that. She is not!"

"Yes, that's what they're saying."

I rode my bike back home, falling and getting up several times as I went. I was frantic and worried. It's a potent memory for me, how I kept slipping and falling. I got home and saw Sven-Arne, his face swollen from crying. "Have you heard what happened?" he asked.

I went into the kitchen. Everyone was crying. Ulla-Britt had just arrived by train, and we gathered in the kitchen.

"Is Anna-Lisa dead?" I asked.

"Yes," answered Mother. "She will never come back again."

Anna-Lisa was on her way to Klippan to buy a dress. She was going to get engaged to her boyfriend, Ingemar, on New Year's Eve and wanted to look extra nice. For advice, she brought her best friend, Siw, with her. Anna-Lisa drove the car, and Siw sat next to her. Anna-Lisa's car skidded in the slippery conditions, and they collided with a milk truck. It killed her instantly. Siw survived but was seriously injured. The man who drove the milk truck knew Anna-Lisa and was appalled by what had happened. It was such a tragedy. Östra Ljungby is a small community, and everyone was affected by the accident.

Father had recently repaired Anna-Lisa's car, so he blamed himself for the accident. He was utterly beside himself with shock and loss. Imagine hearing as a seven-year-old your father screaming and crying. He sometimes screamed during the night, waking us up. It was a horrible time. I was so little and didn't understand.

I remember the funeral. Tina and I were considered too small to wear black, so we got to wear navy blue peacoats. There's a picture of Tina and me where we stood in our coats with flowers in our hands. On the day of the funeral, it snowed over the small church. Father wore a top hat, and the women wore mourning veils over their faces. As a kid, I thought the veils were awful.

"Why do you have those?" I cried. I also remember how we were supposed to look down into the pit when they lowered the coffin.

During the church coffee reception, the pastor, a fantastic man named Carl Greek, distracted us children for a while, and we laughed a bit. It was needed, as we were all scared.

Afterward, everything felt unreal. It was such a damn cold winter. I'd stand with my friends out in the village, feeling how everything was so strange and awful. Quiet, cold, and desolate. The family collapsed when Anna-Lisa died, especially Father, who broke down. My parents seemed to age a decade immediately. Their hair turned gray.

Dad's grief took up all the space. Mother kept her pain inside, and didn't see her cry after the funeral. My older siblings later told me that she'd obsess over how she'd scolded Anna-Lisa the night before the accident. Anna-Lisa had been playing with Tina and me in the bath and splashed water all over the bathroom. Mother became angry about it, and after the tragedy she kept repeating, "Why didn't I let them play? It was just a bit of water. Why did it matter?"

She began to start saying things like, "Let the children do whatever they want. You never know if they'll be able to tomorrow." She didn't want anything postponed, as one would never know when it might be too late.

My father struggled with alcohol before the accident, but he began drinking even more after the funeral. He couldn't look at a single picture of Anna-Lisa without sobbing. Mother removed all the images of my sister from the house to help him. She instructed us not to remind him of our sister or her accident. We weren't supposed to talk about her at all. No pictures of her, no talking about her. It was as if we were pretending she never existed.

But I wanted to talk! My beloved big sister died, and we weren't supposed to mention her? It took several years after the accident before we could openly talk within the family about Anna-Lisa's death.

Today I love to see pictures of Anna-Lisa. I saw so little of her as a child. When Ulla-Britt and Anna-Lisa went out dancing on Saturday nights, I'd watch them put on makeup and get ready. They wore tulle skirts that stood straight out. It was so cool. I wish I had more memories than I have.

Back then, Dad cried, drank, and smoked in the basement. Sometimes I'd creep downstairs and ask, "Dad, what are you doing?" He'd dry his tears as best he could, and we'd sit and talk awhile, mostly about singing and music. He always had the violin with him.

My father was devastated, and it was up to us to try to cheer him up with music. If Tina and I were singing in harmony, he was happy. It was calming for him. Music also helped Tina and me. We went to Sunday school where we were also able to sing. What a relief to be there. It was comforting to sing in the choir on Christmas after the accident.

I could talk to Sven-Arne's wife about Anna-Lisa's death. Gertie and I were close. She came into the family early. I was only a few years old when she and Sven-Arne got married. Gertie once told me that the first thing I said when I saw her was, "Why do you have such a small mouth?" I wasn't timid as a child, but rather was totally straightforward.

Things we'd once argued over as a household lost their significance. Tina swears the family learned to hug after Anna-Lisa's death. A kind of unity emerged, even though we wouldn't or couldn't put it into words. Mother became extra determined to take care of us and suppressed her grief. Sometimes I think her bottled-up grief caused her to be diagnosed with Parkinson's disease at only forty-eight years old.

Tina and I switched off to cope. We went into our dreams and our imaginations. I lived in my fantasies, and went into my fairytale world where I was famous. Ulla-Britt played the reporter, using the handle of her jump rope as a microphone:

"What's your name?"

"Gun-Marie Fredriksson."

"Where do you live?"

"In Östra Ljungby."

No one could get to me in those fantasies. Everything was free and fine. I loved it. Tina and I built our worlds and played everything possible. We watched the whole world through our television and knew there wasn't much happening in Östra Ljungby. Knowing there was a larger world out there made life easier for us.

When I was ten years old, I made my first real friend. Her name was Kerstin, and we borrowed my father's things to play "mail" together. Or we would play "the spirit of the glass," and Tina would join us. We made our own Ouija board. We'd heat a glass with the help of a candle and put our index and middle fingers on the glass while we asked a question. The question could be about a guy or more occult things we wondered about. The glass moved on its own to different letters or numbers — at least, we wanted to believe that was the case. We'd give ourselves quite the fright! Once, the glass flew and crashed to the ground. We made ourselves so scared that we'd be screaming by the end.

Kerstin had the most beautiful laugh in the world. As soon as she laughed, I was happy too. I miss her laughter to this day.

My father was a nice person, but he had a hard life. There were disagreements with his siblings after the bankruptcy about constant financial problems. His continuous hard work for income was never quite enough, and then there was the grief over Anna-Lisa.

I was ashamed when he drank and grew rowdy and belligerent. Mother was also embarrassed. After a bender, she'd say, "Now that's over and done with, let's not talk about it anymore. Everything is fine again," and pretended like it was nothing. But in our small community, everyone knew everything about everyone. There was a lot of gossip, and people constantly talked shit about each other.

And we never knew how the alcohol would affect his behavior, either. Sometimes Dad became a happy fiddler. Other times he grew resentful and went and muttered about. And in those moods, it was usually Mother who was the target. But we didn't want to hear about how awful our father thought our mother was. Before Tina and I fell asleep, we might hear that he was drunk, and we'd want to fast forward to morning. In the summer, we played badminton outside until it was so dark we could barely see the ball. We didn't want to go home where Dad was probably drunk again, bellyaching and slamming doors throughout the house.

I loved my father. But when he got drunk, he talked a lot of shit. The anger he carried within him poured out onto my mother. And in the meantime, we children sat and cried. *He wasn't really like that, we told ourselves, not really! Not our kind father who could joke and play!*

My mother always walked away. Sometimes she told him to shut up. But she never snapped back. She waited for it to pass, let him slam the doors until he eventually went down to the basement and played the violin. It was like water off a duck's back.

Mom was amazing. I don't understand how she endured his moods. Her biggest concern was that we'd have enough money and food for all of us. Dad's alcohol cost money, and I think that was her biggest complaint about his drinking.

Sometimes I ask myself what growing up with our parents did to us, their whole business of "let's pretend like that didn't happen, everything is fine." We became the kind of people that feel like we're responsible for everyone's happiness; *There, let's sing a little song, everything will be fine.* Tina wonders if maybe I should've been angry instead.

When I met Micke, he noticed I told childhood stories from a great distance. I talked about Anna-Lisa's death without getting emotional.

He encouraged me to confront and embrace my upbringing with open arms rather than detachment. I'm grateful for that. It has made me feel whole as a human being. I was no longer as restless, as if worries or darkness were chasing me.

It was imprinted during my childhood that everyone should feel good around me. No one should quarrel or be sad. We had a cat named Missan, for example. I couldn't have been very old when I got in the middle of a fight between her and another cat. I wanted everything to be all right, for them to make up. But I was clawed to shreds.

Today my family talks more about the things we once tried to smooth over. And I've learned that everything feels easier when you share your experiences with others. You feel less alone. However, it can be difficult to put into practice.

When I recount my childhood in this book, I do so with some hesitation. I'm not ashamed or afraid to speak honestly about how it was in our family. I've freed myself from it. Poverty, alcoholism, why should anyone be ashamed of living through it?

Yet I don't want everything to sound so miserable. We children came out all right because we laughed and sang and played. Because we had each other. Our home was full of love. Friends often came to our house because the atmosphere was warm and loving. Mother was so welcoming, "yes, come in here, welcome," and suddenly there'd be twenty people crowded into our little house. It was comfortable and cozy. Our house was a place where everyone was allowed to be. Mom baked buns and made sure everyone got something to eat. Mom and Dad were also curious about our friends and us and enjoyed listening to us talk about our youthful opinions.

And music weaves through all my fondest memories. How we shared it, rejoiced in it, and came together through it. We often had a lot of fun in the middle of all the misery. Father could be so much fun, and the same with Sven-Arne. Dad built a place in the attic that Tina and I could have to ourselves. The attic was above the kitchen, and when Mother thought we were playing records too loud, she pounded a broomstick on the ceiling. We'd hang out up there, have friends over, and smoke Prince Red cigarettes that we'd stolen from our father. We had a way to make sure our theft wouldn't get noticed. We became experts in organizing the package so that it never looked like a cigarette was missing.

In 1966 my father bought a Tandberg tape recorder on which we recorded music from the radio chart programs the *Top Ten (Tio i Topp)* and *The Evening Stop (Kvällstoppen)*. We also recorded our own songs and theater performances.

When I started primary school, my father rented a piano. It was a smaller piano that didn't have all the octaves. Around 1968 he bought a real piano — a Schimmel — in installments. It was difficult for my mom and dad to get enough money together every month, and it took many years to pay it off.

Having a real piano at home was fantastic and incredibly important for Tina and me. That's how we conducted our pitch ear training. We took Beatles songs or any other song we heard on the radio and sang to them, often in a bit of makeshift English, while playing the piano. Tina was more bound to notes, while I was more freeform. I made my first song as early as five or six years old. The lyrics were about a little gray bird falling. Unfortunately, due to my illness, I don't remember the rest. But during my childhood and my teens, I often sat at the piano composing songs.

I've always found great comfort in nature, ever since I was a child. I love animals, birds, and the sea. I love picking flowers. I didn't have many toys but was outside a lot and preoccupied myself with what I found there. Mom loved the garden. She spent a lot of time working to make her garden blossom. It's from her that I inherited my love of flowers.

Also meaningful to me while growing up was Sven-Arne's son Tony. He's six years younger than me, and I was tasked to babysit him. But we huddled together in the evenings and watched horror movies together. We were so close. So alike. Equally sensitive. We both cried at the sad parts of the movies. To this day, when we see each other, we can share a good cry. He's been a great support during my illness, and so sad about it. We're connected. We mirror each other's feelings and experience what the other feels.

I've always cried easily, and Tina could get annoyed by it. Once, we visited Ulla-Britt, who was eleven years older and had moved to Denmark. We were in our teens and had lived with her for a whole month. After saying goodbye on the train platform, I cried all the way home. Tina finally sputtered: "Do you have to cry all the time?"

But I'm like that. My feelings are on the outside. Crying has always been a way to relieve the pressure for me. It helps me access my emotions. As with cancer, it's been helpful to get the cry out. So much in my childhood was about avoiding feelings and looking happy. I've since learned to use crying to vent.

As a child, I was bold in one situation and very scared and sad in others. I had sudden mood changes. I had those extremes. That's still the case!

During my first three years of school, I had a kindhearted teacher. But when I started fourth grade, I got an evil fucking bitch. I loved school, especially math, but she took that away. "You! You little slouch," she called me when I missed something in math. I lost my self-confidence. I didn't think I was good enough anymore, and it gradually got worse. I still carry her harsh words, saying that I am lazy and useless. It's so easy to lose self-esteem without the right kind of encouragement in your youth.

Tina helped me with my homework at home, especially the math that I now found difficult and struggled with. Sometimes, Tina wrote in the correct answers when I was tired. We didn't consider that her handwriting was different from mine. Of course the teacher quickly noticed, and she scolded me for it. I was so ashamed.

It was a different time when I was growing up. Children were treated differently. It was common for children to be hit at home. Some of my playmates were severely beaten by their parents. Mother was the strictest with us. It wasn't fun to receive a smack, but we were used to it. She'd also tap us on the head with a knuckle when she was angry. But for the most part, she was a loving mother.

My father beat me once. I was seven or eight, playing outside with a friend. I came home covered in mud from head to toe, and my father was furious. His anger scared me, so I fled into the house, up to my room. He ran after me and walloped me. I got an ass-whooping. But oh, how he regretted it afterward! He asked for forgiveness and was beside himself with regret.

My parents had different roles. My father was the fiddler with a song for the accordion or violin. Mother kept everything neat, tidy, and in order. She was in charge of the money and made sure to make ends meet. Dad had a more frivolous attitude, believing that things would always turn out fine. If Tina or I wanted money, we went to Dad. He gave it to us if he had any, which made Mom mad sometimes. She was responsible for holding it together. She had the housekeeping money in a special cupboard, and sometimes we stole a few pennies. As teenagers, we also stole Dad's bottle of schnapps and refilled it with water.

It was nice to be a teenager, to enter another world that was a bit more ours and ours alone. Tina and I were always together and had so much fun. Even though I was three years younger than them, I hung out with her and her friends Bitte and Boel. I wanted to be a part of everything they did. I was sort of their mascot, always acting the clown. Like when Tina and her girlfriends had a Christmas party, and I dressed up as a Christmas elf and put on a comedy show for them. Or when we went to earn some extra money by picking strawberries. I stood among the plants, hamming it up until they writhed with laughter. The foreman got angry because we laughed until we fell to the ground, smashing the strawberries.

Sometimes they teased me and weren't always the nicest. Once they made me crawl under the sofa, and I wasn't allowed to come out until I'd sung "Du Gamla, Du Fria" (the Swedish national anthem) in its entirety. They sat on the couch and blocked me from getting out with their legs. Another time, when I was a few years old, they cut my long hair just before Sven-Arne's wedding, and my mother had put in a lot of effort trying to make it look good.

But for the most part, we had fun.

When I was thinking about who I was as a teenager, I found this . . . *(Marie shows her copy of 'My Diary')*. I was probably thirteen when I wrote in it:

Clothes I like: long trousers with cuffs, polo jumpers, patterned pants, midi-coat, fringe vest, burgundy knickers, V-jeans, sweater with lacing, white boots.

Good books: Children 312.

Friends: Lotta, Bitte, Eva-Karin. Very cool and super friendly.

My idols: Creedence, Pugh Rogefeldt, Led Zeppelin, the Stones, Jimi Hendrix, Ike and Tina Turner . . .

I was down with what was popular back then. Tina and I found Radio Luxembourg on the radio. It was so great to hear the music they played. A whole new wonderful world! Ulla-Britt gave us our first vinyl single, and it was the Monkees. We were ecstatic. We started buying records, and we lived for these 45s. When it was hard at home, we got lost in them. We bought singles of the Beatles and the Rolling Stones. The first single I bought with my own money was "Valleri" by the Monkees.

We also continued listening to the *Top Ten* and *The Evening Stop*. We cried when we heard Moody Blues sing "Night in White Satin" because it was so beautiful. Deep Purple and Led Zeppelin were also influential to me. I've always been drawn to a harder sound when it comes to music. Jimi Hendrix, for example. I adored him.

For Tina and me, pop was our music. For my father, modern music was nothing but thumping; he didn't understand it. When it came to pop and rock, Father stayed out of it.

It was liberating to enter the teenage world, but times were rocky when I was twelve or thirteen. I spent a lot of time goofing off and smoking. I couldn't keep up in school. I did well in drawing, music, and gymnastics, but I had pretty low grades in the other subjects.

Oh, and the smoking, the constant smoking. We smoked incessantly in our home. Everyone smoked except my mother. We'd all try to get her to smoke on New Year's Eve. She'd puff and cough, and we thought it was hilarious. We loved how much she didn't like it. Today it sounds completely absurd. What were we thinking?

During my early teens, I felt demands on myself that I couldn't cope with. At the same time, I wasn't lost in what direction I wanted my life to take. I knew what I wanted to be very early on: an actress or singer. I wanted high heels and fancy hairstyles. Hollywood, my God! To reach those heights was a dizzying thought!

Katharine Hepburn became my role model early on. I admired the masculine style she cultivated. In the beginning, with Roxette, I often wore a dress or short skirt onstage, but little by little, I found I preferred a suit or trousers. A rock look; stylish, a little masculine.

When we started going out with friends, Tina and I hitchhiked to Helsingborg. We couldn't afford anything better. Sometimes we hitched with rather unsavory individuals. We'd often exit the car early because the driver seemed creepy, and it was pure luck that nothing terrible happened. Once, we took the ferry over to Denmark with friends, bought cherry wine, and divided it four ways. We quickly became very drunk and dropped the bottle. It broke into a thousand pieces, and the rest of the wine ran out on the sidewalk. It was probably for the best.

Since I hung out with Tina and she was older, I experimented early. I drank and smoked. Tina and Boel were fifteen when they started smoking in secret; I was only twelve. At first, they forced me to smoke so that I wouldn't tell on them. If I was in on it, they knew I'd keep quiet.

We also went to the Basement Club in Klippan when I was twelve. There I heard James Brown for the first time, his song "Sex Machine." It was fantastic. I just died. It was like a message from the bigger world. A guy who had hay sticking out of his clogs even asked me to dance. He'd just come straight from a barn.

When did I start to feel like I had something special?

I had vocal power. I knew I could sing loud and strong. Tina and I sang in the children's choir every Sunday, and it was clear how robust my voice was. Quite early on, I also noticed that I touched people when I sang. My voice evoked emotion in them.

My sisters think that Dad knew I'd turn out to be a singer, even though he never wanted to favor me over the others. When Tina saw me singing in the high school choir, she said I had something special. We sang gospel, and everyone stood still except me, who moved to the music. I drew eyes my way, she said. I had a noticeable charisma.

There's a lot of darkness in my childhood history, yet many moments I remember with warmth. They're like my little treasures that I can recall when I need some happiness. Like when Mother drove Tina and me to Råbocka camping on hot summer days to swim. Just the three of us, a blanket to sit on, and a packed picnic basket. We spent all day there; smooth sand, blue sea, blue sky. We had many joyful and fun times. Like when we got a tent. We set it up in the garden, and Tina and I sat inside with our friends, telling secrets to each other and giggling. These are the moments I cradle close to me, and no one can take them away.

My father died when he was sixty-seven, his third heart attack. Dad thought salad was rabbit food, spread butter on the cinnamon buns, and always over-salted food. My mother died when she was seventy-five. Their hard life, full of bad food, stress, and grief took its toll. But they did have some great years together after retirement — less worries and stress. Dad had joked about how he'd found his apron and often stood by the stove. And Mother finally got some peace and quiet.

Dad, unfortunately, didn't get to be part of my breakthrough as an artist. But recently, during my Swedish tour, I dedicated the song "If You Saw Me Now" to him. I always think of him when I sing it:

If you saw me now	*Om du såg mig nu*
Would you dare to believe in me?	*Skulle du våga tro på mej?*
You know I miss you	*Du vet jag saknar dej*
If you saw me now	*Om du såg mej nu*
when I got a bit on my way	*när jag kommit en bit på väg*
No doubt in my step	*Ingen tvekan i mitt steg*
if you came, if you saw,	*om du kom, om du såg,*
Here I am . . .	*här är jag . . .*
And I'll never forget what you said	*Och jag glömmer aldrig det du sa*
you are still here	*du finns kvar*
and I remember you as the friend you were	*och jag minns dig som den vän du var*
you always had time for me	*du hade alltid tid för mig*
I always had time for you	*jag hade alltid tid för dig*
If you saw me now	*Om du såg mig nu*
Would you dare to believe in me?	*Skulle du våga tro på mig?*
You know I miss you	*Du vet jag saknar dig*
If you saw me now	*Om du såg mig nu*

when I got a bit on my way
no doubt in my step
If you came, if you saw,
you disappeared . . .

Like a bird from a desolate beach
in my hand
all the words I never found
And I'll never forget,
That our time can be so short
If you saw me now . . .

när jag kommit en bit på väg
ingen tvekan i mitt steg
Om du kom, om du såg,
du försvann . . .

Som en fågel från en öde strand
i min hand
alla ord jag aldrig någonsin fann
Och jag ska aldrig glömma bort,
Att vår tid kan vara så kort
Om du såg mig nu . . .

CHAPTER 4

"Suddenly, the equations added up."

In Marie's words.

———

A fter primary school, I started a two-year economics program. I felt uncomfortable immediately. Economics? What was I thinking? I couldn't even keep track of my own money. Admittedly, there was hardly any to keep track of, but still.

It was probably the only program I was able to get accepted to, as my grades weren't that great. I wanted to attend the music high school in Malmö, but I didn't stand a chance at doing that, I thought. So, I did my best in the financial program for the first year.

The only part of high school that I liked was singing in the choir. Once when we were going to sing the Beatles song "Yesterday," I was chosen to lead. Afterward, several people came up and complimented me, mentioning that I should make a go of singing. I wasn't yet brave enough to imagine supporting myself as a singer. It was ingrained from home that I needed to pick a safe and secure career.

I tried to come up with alternatives. Maybe I could become a singing tutor? I could make a living from that. But I wanted to be a singer, not a tutor. So, I told the school's guidance counselor . . . and was taken seriously!

After searching all over Sweden, the counselor found a newly-started music program at Fridhem's folk high school in Svalöv. It was also quite close to Östra Ljungby. I had to apply and audition, so I went and showed them what I was capable of. Technically I was too young to attend, as you were supposed to be eighteen and I was only seventeen. However, I sang so well at the audition that they made an exception. I was one of eight students accepted that year, and I finally felt at home in a school environment. The two years that followed changed my life. I began to take music (and myself) seriously. Svalöv also vastly improved my self-confidence, as I'd come from little Östra Ljungby to make music with adult musicians from different parts of the country. Can you imagine?

I was quickly singled out as a talented singer with a unique voice. I remember singing the Mamas & the Papas' song "Dream a Little Dream of Me" in class, and everybody cheered wildly and told me how terrific the performance was. They also started to give me an increasing number of solos during programs. I started to assert myself, and strived to use my voice correctly and make it more my own. The other students played instruments — some were great on guitar, some on bass. I played the piano but mainly took the role of the singer. We had eight students in the class, three girls and five boys, and we became somewhat of a band.

My musical interests grew, blues and jazz, Ella Fitzgerald, Aretha Franklin, and Billie Holiday. Their singing styles inspired me. There was something so freeing about jazz, and improvisation had always been close to my heart. When I sing, I go right into my feelings, and anything can come out. These influences helped me regain my self-confidence, allowing me to study seriously. We also learned English and math at school, and I was assigned a great teacher who made math fun. I finally solved equations that I hadn't been able to solve before, because the teacher was so damn good.

I lived at the school during the week and went home on weekends. At home, I ate homemade meals, and before each new week, my mother gave me a hundred kroner ($11) to live off. I felt so grown-up and proud when I sat with the hundred kroner note in my hand on the train back to school.

One day the whole class came to my house in Östra Ljungby. Oh, that was a big deal. Mother and Father generously left the house so that we could be alone. Tina joined us, as well as my best friends back home, Kerstin, Eva-Karin, and Christel. We drank beer and played and sang. It was such a great feeling to have all these friends having fun at my house! I was so proud.

The theater was the only thing I'd considered doing besides music. There was a theater program at the folk high school, and I had some friends there. Sometimes I helped the theater students with music for their plays. Actor Peter Haber and director Peter Oskarson came to the school to look for extras for the Skånska Teatern theater company. I made sure to make myself visible. I got to go to Landskrona and improvise so that they could see how I managed onstage. They were so happy with my performance that they even gave me a line or two. I was supposed to say, "You are not allowed to travel!"

The play was *Maria från Borstahusen* by Mary Andersson. It took place in a poor neighborhood during the turn of the century, and we performed the play in Landskrona. We got to wear such nice stage clothes, long skirts and narrow waists. I loved being onstage. I felt at home there. And I wanted to stand in the front. This has been the case ever since I was little. All my fantasies and playtime revolved around it; I pictured myself center stage, whether it was music or theater.

During the years I've been ill, I've been inclined to hide, which isn't like me. My Swedish tour for *Now!* was like therapy. I just had to get out there and be on stage again! I'm ecstatic that the desire to do so is back. The joy of being onstage makes me *me*; it's a part of my identity.

The play went on tour around the country, and that's how I came to Stockholm for the first time. The subway was entirely new for me. I was terrified because the trains traveled so fast, and it was stressful to board on time. The doors opened and closed so rapidly. I called my mother, eager to tell her about the subway and the escalators. And it was probably right then when I decided I wanted to live in Stockholm.

The highlight of Stockholm was that [Swedish Prime Minister] Olof Palme came and watched the show. My mother and father respected him. At home, we often talked about him and his ideas. He came backstage and greeted the ensemble. We were all dizzy with excitement. It was definitely a moment to call home about!

Up to this time, I still hadn't decided whether to continue with acting or music. But in Stockholm, I realized I couldn't live without singing. The need was deeply rooted within me. It was the part of me I believed in the most.

In the second year at school, a new class arrived, and some of the close, intimate atmosphere disappeared. I stayed for two years. Today, the folk high school in Svalöv is very popular, and I'm proud to have been one of the first students to attend.

At a concert with Supertramp at Olympen in Lund, I met Stefan Dernbrant. He came from Åled outside Halmstad and worked at Tempo [a department store]. Stefan was as interested in music as I was. He liked jazz and experimental music, such as Yes. And that's how we connected.

We were quite different. He was down-to-earth and stable, while I was chaotic and flighty. His family was friendly, albeit a bit reserved.

I was straightforward and emotionally driven and was used to a much louder and more impulsive family. Stefan said I introduced hugging to his family. They didn't embrace before I came into the picture.

Stefan was my first big love, a bighearted person, soft and sweet. We bonded over music, playing the flute together and trying the saxophone. My friends from school accepted him and my parents immediately liked him. We went to London for a week together — the capital of pop! It was extraordinary. I'm not sure how we could afford it. The taxis were nerve-racking; you were supposed to understand how to pay instantly. I was twenty-one and had flown for the first time, having never been abroad except to Denmark.

After folk high school, I wasn't exactly sure what to do next. Luckily, Stefan was quite organized, and we moved in together in Halmstad. Stefan played drums in a band called Strulpojkarna. Per and Mats "MP" Persson occasionally accompanied them before they became too busy with Gyllene Tider [a popular Swedish group]. Martin Sternhufvud was the group's leader. He played guitar and sang lead vocals.

One day he heard me sitting at the piano, singing a song that I had written, and began asking me to join the group. I wanted to but felt unsure. Stefan also pestered me. They both thought that I sang and played the piano so well.

I felt confused about my situation. What was I supposed to do with my life? I felt lost in the newness of being a young woman in a big city. And I needed to keep coming up with ways to earn an income. I took various odd jobs, once as a gardener, and then as a nursing home employee. I also tried to attend municipal adult education, but quickly gave that up. I used unemployment benefits between jobs and sometimes found work through government work programs.

One of those jobs was at a café in Halmstad called Tre Hjärtan, a trendy place where waitresses had to wear tight black skirts, white shirts, and high heels. The idea was to look like a real lady, and I hadn't dressed that way before. The guests were high-end and dressed well. The owners were quite kind, and it was wonderful to finally make some money. Once I dropped a whole plate of buns, *smack*, right on the floor. I was so anxious about keeping my job that I picked them up and served them as if nothing had happened. Thankfully no one got angry, and the guests chuckled at my mishap.

Eventually, I became one of the members of the band Strulpojkarna, which was renamed Strul. Martin suggested that I write my own songs to lead, while he would compose and sing his own songs as well. One of our first gigs was at the Kattegat School in Halmstad in front of 400 people. The day after, the local newspaper headline read, *Strul's performance was good, thanks to Marie.* I saved that article.

Martin and I continued to write additional songs. I listened a lot to Heart, Ricki Lee Jones, and Pat Benatar and wanted to emulate their sound. I did a lot of *screaming* vocals during this period.

I met several creative people through Stefan who came to mean a lot to me over the years: Ika Nord, with whom I would eventually tour; Uffe Andreasson, who would later become my assistant during the Roxette era; and Maggan Ek, who did theater. Maggan wondered if I would write music for a play she had made called *Attractive Attitudes (Attraktiva attityder)*. I played a small role in the production, made mood music, and added some songs to the plot.

In the play, I sang "As Time Goes By." Bertil Frisk from Nizzan Jazzband heard the song and asked if I wanted to sing with them. The members were slightly older, and they played traditional jazz.

We toured around a lot and played at Stampen [a Swedish jazz bar] in Stockholm, among other places. I earned a few hundred in one night. The usual fee was $35 (300 SEK) and free beer. Once we played at Halmstad's golf club, I received $90 (800 SEK) directly in my pocket. I'll never forget that. It was so much money at the time.

Prog and alternative music were popular during this time. I wasn't used to discussing politics, but I started to take a stand on everything. I dressed like a hippie with long hair and long dresses. I begged an acquaintance for an old, dirty Afghan fur that was disgusting, but I felt cool and individualistic when I wore it. My siblings begged me to throw it away because it smelled like hell.

The coolest thing to me from this time were pictures and film from the Woodstock music festival. It made me think about music in a new way, that music could change the world and bring people together for peace and love. The music was freeing and encouraged everyone to be exactly whatever they wanted. It was very political.

There was an alternative festival in Halmstad, but we weren't allowed to participate. So we decided to create something similar, which became the Strul Festival. I think the first festival was in 1979, and several local bands participated.

Martin was determined to get a recording contract. We were the ones who had time because we were both unemployed, so we went to Stockholm and badgered various record companies, while Stefan remained in Halmstad and worked.

I was so restless back then. I wanted to stay one step ahead, which led to inevitable and painful breakups. I fell in love with Martin, and we felt guilty hurting Stefan the way we did. It quickly became untenable to stay in the same band.

As we were about to break up the band, things started to happen. Strul was offered to release a single. It was fantastic news, but I felt terrible for Stefan. I asked him to remain and create the single with us, but he didn't want to. Martin and I recorded "Ki-i-ai-oo/Strul Igen" with other musicians.

There were also offers from television. *Rockcirkus* was a program recorded at Cirkus [a concert venue] in Stockholm. But a few weeks before our first appearance, Sven-Arne called and said my father had suddenly died. He suffered a heart attack at home at the kitchen table on April 20, 1981. I went to Ängelholm, where Tina was, and we both then traveled to Östra Ljungby. It was difficult for my mother, who was also dealing with Parkinson's. And I was sad that my father never got to see me sing as an artist.

Martin and I still agreed to appear on *Rockcirkus*. Bertil Goldberg was the emcee, and I kicked everything off, full throttle, with the lyric *"I'm alone, I'm alone, but I know my ability! (Ensam, ensam är jag men jag vet min kapacitet!)."* [The material with Strul] wasn't my own, and when I look at it now, I don't think it was my style. My family sat in the front of the show with signs that said *Strul*. They were always there for me, my number one supporters. I still get choked up thinking about it.

Despite Strul recording a single, not much else happened. [Local band] Gyllene Tider likewise hadn't had their breakthrough yet. But they had a lovely, tidy rehearsal studio with carpeting halfway up the walls. Strul rented the adjacent room, which looked like a regular rehearsal studio — a big mess full of beer cans and cigarette butts.

Martin and I went on to form the group MaMas Barn. We wanted to make it clear that we were on a new path. Anders Herrlin and Micke "Syd" Andersson from Gyllene Tider promised to record with us.

Martin and I eventually moved in with a collective living quarter in Steninge, outside Halmstad.

Per Gessle, then still of Gyllene Tider, thought I hung out a bit too much with hippie crowds. He liked pop; I liked blues and rock. I thought Per was a bit of a mama's boy. He had money and was a neat freak. His records were always in perfect order. We liked to tease him by changing their order, and he'd go completely crazy. It was the exact opposite of me, who had nothing in order.

Even though Per and I were so different, we found each other in the music. You know what song we met over? It was "Tin Soldier" by Small Faces.

"Isn't it good?"

"Yes, it's the best song ever!"

I love that Per and I understood each other through that song. We were both completely taken by it. We gushed over how amazing it was.

Eventually, I also sang with Per on a Christmas record that came with the magazine *Schlager*. You know, a free bonus single. This was in December 1981 in a studio in Getinge. It was a Gyllene Tider song called "Nothing of What You Need (Ingenting av vad du behöver)." I thought it was very cool. Per's band Gyllene Tider had become the most popular group in Sweden at that time, and we always had such a good feeling when we created something together.

The highlight of MaMas Barn during those years was when we got to play at the rock club Ritz in Stockholm. Micke Syd played drums, Anders Herrlin was on bass, Nalle Bondesson and Martin played the guitar, and I sang while playing the electric grand piano and choir organ. I wore a black dress and felt very cool and absolutely in the right place. In retrospect, I found out that Micke [my future husband] was in the audience, and he thought I looked like a cool chick.

MaMas Barn also got to be on the television show *Electric Garden* (*Elektriska trädgården*), presenting new music from a live stage in Stockholm.

Martin probably always thought of Gyllene Tider as a prototype [for MaMas Barn]. Maybe not the band's sound as much as their success. We wanted to become successful, and we saw it was possible. Making an album with MaMas Barn was a main goal. We first tried to get EMI on board, but Kjell Andersson [A&R] didn't think it was quite finished. He liked my singing style but wasn't sure about Martin and me together. Eventually, we got a record deal with Metronome.

As lost as I've felt in life, I've always felt an enormous strength when I sing. No human in the world can take it away from me. During the creation of the record, my emotions fluctuated dramatically. Either I was exuberantly happy or sitting alone in a corner and crying. Martin was bursting with ideas. Incredibly creative. But he was also dominant. He took over, while I found it increasingly difficult to find myself in what we were doing.

The record we ended up making wasn't very successful. Martin was unhappy with the first mix, so we redid everything to make it sound a little tougher. We were probably a bit difficult to work with.

The MaMas Barn album received some good reviews but sold just under a thousand copies. Martin thought we should continue working together. None of us were happy with the record's production, and Martin thought we should try again to show what we were capable of.

I received offers for solo recording contracts with both Metronome and EMI. The allure to stop hiding as part of a band and step forward on my own was tempting. Yet I felt like I was betraying Martin. I called my mother and asked for advice.

"You'll probably do the right thing, as long as you don't end up in some drug den," she said.

I had met Lasse Lindbom, producer for Gyllene Tider, on a few occasions. Niklas Strömstedt played with Lasse then, and he tipped off Lasse about me. I went to Stockholm and sang a duet with Lasse, a song called "So Close Now (Så nära nu)." This was 1983. I was so nervous that I hid in the bathroom and breathed deeply until I could calm myself down. Lasse and Niklas both told me that they'd thought I'd locked myself in the toilet to smoke some weed. I was completely off due to performance anxiety.

Even while working with MaMas Barn, Lasse talked about wanting to write songs with me and produce me as a solo artist. He wasn't alone. By then, I had a choice between Metronome and working with Anders Burman and Mats Ronander, or EMI, where Rolf Nygren, Kjell, and Lasse were. Per asserted that EMI was cooler and that I'd feel more at home there. So I agreed to a record contract at EMI as a solo artist. Mine and Martin's relationship ended around this time. It was hard, and I felt a bit deceitful. But it was time for me to make my voice heard.

CHAPTER 5

At Marie's Home in Djursholm
(in the studio in the attic).
September, 2014.

It's a crisp, clear autumn day. The hum of leaf blowers all around us drifts through the gardens in Marie's neighborhood. Manicured lawns freed from the cover of rust-colored leaves glow juicy green in the sun.

Inside the villa, Marie is happy and full of expectations. Clarence Öfwerman, Per, and Christoffer have come to visit. Two new Roxette songs will be recorded in the studio that Marie and Micke built on the top floor of their house. The foundation tracks have been laid, and only Marie's vocals are missing.

Up in the attic studio, Studio Vinden, hangs a large portrait of Joni Mitchell. Marie says she adores it, not just because it's beautiful and frames one of her biggest idols, but also because it was a gift from Per and Åsa after the last tour. The gang slowly fills in. Soon a new world tour will begin with a premiere in Vladivostok and then ten more Russian cities: Khabarovsk, Krasnoyarsk, Novosibirsk, Magnitogorsk, Yekaterinburg, Saratov, Rostov-on-Don, Krasnodar, St. Petersburg, and finally, Moscow.

Roxette has played in Russia many times and has a large fanbase there. It is the fans with whom they have a mutually warm relationship. The people, as Marie often puts it. We play for the people. It's them that we care about.

The last few times that Marie and I have seen each other, she's expressed concern regarding the tour start date. Her foot has been acting up lately. During the Swedish tour, she began appearing on-stage barefoot to reduce the cramping in her foot and create more stability.

She started getting Botox injections in her leg in an attempt to reduce the cramps. It's helped, but Marie thinks her foot and balance are getting worse. She's still uncertain if it will work. None of the doctors know exactly what's happening but concur it's probably a result of the heavy amount of radiation her brain has been subjected to. The injury causes swelling, which puts pressure on parts of her brain. She's looked at me with tear-filled eyes several mornings, questioning whether she'll be able to do it.

What if this doesn't work? What if I can't do it? What if I fall? Her eyes search mine for answers.

Yet once Marie airs the questions out loud, her voice firms with conviction, and she's strong enough to wipe away her tears with a slightly trembling hand. "I'll make it work. It has to work." She shrugs. "In the worst case, I guess we'll have to cancel. Or I'll fall. Whatever will be, will be. Looking at the bigger picture, it's a small problem."

I now know the path Marie's anxiety takes in the face of each new challenge. The fear, the tears, the hard-set firmness, and then an almost frivolous shrug. Whatever is possible is possible. Or it's not.

Still, it's impossible to ignore how the anxiety is always there, right next to her. How she's often fighting at the outer limits of her ability and yet achieves moments of success that otherwise seemed impossible.

She's simply a great fighter.

Learning new lyrics is a challenge for Marie nowadays. Songs are recorded verse by verse, over and over. Sometimes the words are forgotten. Sometimes they are misspoken. Sometimes the expression is wrong. It's common to record music line by line today, with the technology available. But with Marie's insecurity regarding learning new lyrics, the process can be tedious.

Meanwhile, Per sits on a sofa and communicates with fans via Roxette's website. He does this every day. The contact between Roxette and the fans is lively and faithful. How many likes did they get today? And how many times does he go on to check? Per admits, albeit in a lighthearted tone, that he's been bit by "click-addiction." He doesn't want to reflect too deeply upon it.

Instead, he shares pictures of fans with tattooed lines from Roxette songs on their bodies. His lyrics are engraved on the skin of people worldwide. Like so much that has to do with Roxette — the evidence of their impact is staggering.

The coffee machine hums, and cinnamon buns and fruit are out on the table. Clarence sits next to Christoffer by the mixing table, but Christoffer handles the technology. Clarence listens and sometimes comments. He's been Roxette's producer since the band started and a crucial part of Roxette's sound.

The new songs are called "Some Other Summer" and "It Just Happens" and are scheduled to be released Christmas 2015 or at the beginning of 2016. "Some Other Summer" is more of a disco tune, sounding akin to the Pet Shop Boys. "It Just Happens" is a ballad of the kind that Roxette has had such success with over the years, such as "It Must Have Been Love," "Vulnerable," and "Spending My Time."

Per has clear memories of Marie from their time as neighbors in the rehearsal studios in Halmstad. His memory agrees with what Marie recalls of the first time they met.

"She was a pretty wild girl. I lived in a safe middle-class home with my mother, a housewife, and my father, a plumber. It wasn't a rich home, but it was solid and clean. Marie moved into a sketchy prog-collective with Martin. I still lived in my childhood room and loved glam rock, punk, and Patti Smith. The music scene in Halmstad was strictly political, and I never really liked Swedish prog music. They gave me shit for not joining in, but no one in Gyllene Tider was interested in politics. I also don't know how deep in it Marie was. She was in one of those prog groupings. She had friends who went to Christiania to buy weed, and I wasn't into that. Or I guess I wanted to, but my mom wouldn't let me. But what I especially remember about Marie is that she sang so damn well. I've always thought so."

Per especially remembers one such moment. "I heard her in Radio Halland's studio. She recorded her acoustic songs, and I was astounded by her compositions. A song called "It's Hard to Break Up (Det är svårt att bryta upp)" later appeared on MaMas Barn's record. Marie on the piano was magical."

Per sounds so taken when he describes the sight and memory of her. But like Marie, he says there's never been any romance between them. They've been more like siblings. When he got his apartment in Halmstad, they often hung out at his place and watched *Dallas* or *Dynasty* while drinking wine.

"We've never been in love, but we've always completely trusted each other. You can compare what Marie and I have with a romantic relationship in some ways. When I wrote the lyrics for 'It Must Have Been Love,' I wanted it to be about finding a life partner who makes you a little better than you are," he says. "And the same can be said about Marie and me. Musically, we make each other a little better than we are."

And their collaboration was undeniably the beginning of something magnificent. "I was surprised that Marie wanted to form Roxette with me. She was such a star, and I was a twenty-five-year-old has-been," he admits. "I wanted her to stay with me. I did what I could to make her feel comfortable. Marie sang, and I wrote the songs. Those were our roles. She wrote one or two songs for each record. She was the stand-out in the band, and I became the hit machine while she remained the face. In the beginning, she was always given the Roxette suite [by promoters], while I was the one carrying the guitar and being told to wait in the cafeteria. Everyone thought she *was* Roxette, like a solo star, and I was someone along for the ride."

Per points out many differences between Marie's and his music preferences. Marie likes a little more advanced and challenging music. Her roots are in prog music, with "long songs and a lot of fingers on the piano keys," preferably with roots in blues and jazz. She's not a "pop girl" and hadn't taken pop seriously before Roxette came into her life.

"The more poppy the Roxette songs have been, the harder it's been to get Marie on board. For example, she likes Jimi Hendrix, who symbolizes the blues chords I have difficulty with. I get quite cold when faced with big, complicated chords often found in what I call 'adult music,' like Steve Winwood or Billy Joel. I'm more single-minded like the Ramones and the classic pop school," Per says. "Our musical heritage is different in several ways. I try to use it to our benefit. When I make a song, I ask her to use her musical intuition, don't sing it like I'm doing on the demo. The same goes for the songs she composes that I've written lyrics to, like 'Watercolors in the Rain' [on the *Joyride* LP]. It's amazing. I couldn't have written that music."

"Per, come and listen."

Clarence wants Per's attention. They're listening to the recording of "It Just Happens." Everyone agrees that it sounds good. After a short coffee break, they continue with the recording of "Some Other Summer." Stanza after stanza. Take after take. Marie praises Christoffer's patience, how he never seems to get tired. He can record forever without his upbeat mood disappearing.

"It's so hard for me to memorize lyrics," says Marie. "I've had to work hard on the latest Roxette records, but in the end, it works. Christoffer has such tremendous patience."

Christoffer says that he, for his part, believes it's Marie who has the patience. "I don't think she realizes the energy that comes with meeting a person like her," he says.

"The power you get from being with a person who continues to fight the way she does."

And when Per points out that Per and Marie are better together than they are separate, Christoffer agrees. "Together, they're an artist who manages to communicate with millions and millions of people worldwide. I've seen people of all ages and cultures cry uncontrollably when Marie interprets Per's music and lyrics. Despite their unique talents, they don't have that power individually."

Finally, the song comes out right. Marie exits the studio, cheeks red with delight. A big smile breaks out on her face as she utters Roxette's absolute favorite expression: "Woo-hoo!"

She adds, "I'm so happy when we're up and running! When I'm not just a diagnosis!"

CHAPTER 6

"I always wanted to move on."

Marie opens up about her solo career.

I came to EMI to make my first solo record with Lasse as producer. Pretty soon, we also became a couple. I still lived in Halmstad, on Rotorpshöjden, and often in Lasse's studio apartment in
Blåsut. We lived for music. We talked about music and made music
around the clock. Work and leisure flowed together.

My first album, *Hot Wind* (*Het vind*) in 1984, ended up a very scat-
tered record. The album plays like we're searching for a sound. We
put "There's Still a Scent of Love" near the end of the playlist, as
neither Lasse nor I had any real feelings for it. The record company
executives wanted to make it into a single. We were doubtful, and
I thought it was too weak. But the record company was right. "There's
Still a Scent of Love" was a huge hit. Today I am proud of it; it's
touched many people.

We were inspired by Cyndi Lauper when we recorded *Hot Wind*.
We have a Swedish version of "All Through the Night" called "Natt
efter natt." Martin also wrote a song for the album, "I Will Give
Everything (Jag ska ge allt)." I know he went to the states on the money
he made.

After *Hot Wind* I toured as a solo artist for the first time, in thir-
ty-five cities. I wasn't used to standing alone on a stage, and Ika Nord
came along to support me. She'd gone to mime school in Paris,
which always impressed me. She was charismatic and helped me with
makeup, choreography, and outfits. Onstage, she sang backup and
danced. We had a lot of fun together.

Guitarist Staffan Astner also came along for the tour. Both Micke and I have continued to work with him. He was with Micke in the home studio when I had the seizure and fainted in the bathroom. Leffe Larsson played keyboard, Pelle Syrén bass, Pelle Andersson was on drums, and Nane Kvillsäter guitar. Bosse "BoJo" Johansson was our tour leader back then, and Roxette's now. He's my rock when we're traveling.

Ika and I shared a room. She did my makeup, and we'd blow out our eighties hairstyles together. Ika was a skilled performance artist and at ease onstage in a way that I lacked. I was more uncertain about what I should do and how I looked. I felt confident about my music but found myself overwhelmed by everyone's opinions about almost everything else.

Ika listened to me and supported me to be assertive in what I wanted. Our connection was rather uenxpected, since we were quite different. We rarely liked the same books, music, or movies. We did find an overlap in religion and enjoyed discussing it at length. We also shared a similar feeling of experiencing ourselves as an instrument for forces bigger than ourselves.

In 1984 when I played at Glädjehuset in Stockholm, TV cameras recorded the concert. I wore a dress designed by Ika. It was a cubism pattern, artistic with high shoulders, and making it even bolder, one-sleeved. It puzzled some. My mother called my aunt and asked what she thought of my performance.

"Terrible," exclaimed my aunt. "What the heck was Marie wearing? Her dress was unfinished!"

Mom sent regrets that we had only had time to make one sleeve.

A pivotal person I befriended during this time was Efva Attling. She styled me a lot in the beginning. I got my first leather pants from her! She and Marianne Randolph later made the clothes for Rock Around the Kingdom [Rock runt riket, Roxette's first Swedish tour in 1987].

Efva and I became friends around 1981. Gyllene Tider played at the Atlantic in Stockholm, and we were both there. I was singing back-up for Gyllene, and Efva tailored their clothes. She asked if I wanted to head downtown with her and took me to Klippoteket, a hip hair salon, and said, "Here is Marie. She sings fantastically. Now let's fix her hair!" She thought I had nice eyebrows but made sure I cut my bangs. Efva helped me find my style; I was along for the ride. I was nervous but happy once I saw the outcome.

Efva introduced me to various hip people in Stockholm. She visited me in Halmstad during the winter. I had bought a large Russian hat with a cuff from a second-hand shop. I showed it off to her, so proud. Efva once said she'd never forgotten how gorgeous I looked standing on the platform waiting for her train. She thought I looked like I was straight from the movie *Doctor Zhivago*.

We headed to my place on Rotorpshöjden to try to make music together. I placed a tape recorder between us, and Efva had severe performance anxiety. She broke down because she didn't think she could sing. We stopped to eat, and afterward, she washed the dishes with tears rolling down her cheeks. I snapped at her and told her that she had to get herself together. She had to believe in herself. She tearfully agreed, and we made "Let Them Believe (Låt dem tro)," a song about the gossip in Stockholm. Unfortunately, the song wasn't very good. I think we played it only once in Karlstad.

Efva and I still see each other. We usually eat Christmas lunch at NK [department store], a tradition we've kept for thirty years now. We sit and chat, cry, or laugh together. We're both emotional people.

In recent years it's been challenging to make it work since we're not always home over Christmas. But we try.

It was automatically assumed that Lasse and I should make another record together after *Hot Wind*. The expectations from EMI after the hit "There's Still a Scent of Love" were high. With my second album *The Seventh Wave* [1986], I felt that we'd found our unique sound. And with it came my breakthrough.

Lasse and I composed the songs for the album together in the Canary Islands. For six weeks, we stayed in a bungalow on the beach in San Agustín. Lasse laid the foundation for a melody, then I took over, and he continued based on what I had added. It was a real collaboration. We lived every day with that record. We connected through songwriting and thought about music around the clock. We grew so close. But it could be hard to come up for air. Lasse was also nine years older and had a lot more experience.

We finished the songs and recorded the album in EMI's studio. We took care of most things ourselves; the whole album was ours alone. There were only two songs that neither Lasse nor I composed: "For Those Who Love (För dom som älskar)," which Ulf Lundell wrote lyrics and made music for, and "Toward Unknown Seas (Mot okända hav)," written by Ulf Schagerström.

The LP *The Seventh Wave*, with songs like "The Best Day (Den bästa dagen)," title track "The Seventh Wave," and "A House by the Sea (Ett hus vid havet)" exploded. The whole album was a huge hit! I became a recognized artist, in part thanks to Lasse.

I met [longtime manager] Marie Dimberg during this time, and she is an integral part of my life. She worked with PR at EMI. I was standing around, stalling because I had to see 'Lisbeth the Clerk,' the woman at EMI who doled out the checks. I was a bit scared of her. Marie asked if she could come along as moral support. And that's how we got to know each other. She even drove me back and forth between appearances and performances with the press or the audience. I was in the middle of *The Seventh Wave* then. Marie was present when the photographer Calle Bengtsson took the photo for the album cover. There, I'm wearing my hair in a typical eighties style. I was so uncertain back then. I didn't know what to wear or how to look. I became the blond, jeans-n-sweater-girl on my covers.

My relationship with Lasse ended during the recording of *The Seventh Wave*, but we continued our successful music collaborations [to a third album in 1987], even though we no longer were dating. That LP came to be called *After the Storm* (*Efter stormen*). It was an even bigger hit [#1 in Sweden]. This was about the same time that Roxette began.

Per probably thought that *After the Storm* could wait. But at the time I wanted to make another solo record. Many believed that the record was about Lasse's and my separation, something we wanted to get out of our system. But most of the songs were ideas we'd had while we were still together.

The title track, "After the Storm," was the first single. I was so proud of it. I wrote it under a lot of pressure. "If You Could See Me Now (Om du såg mej nu)" and "Just for One Day (Bara för en dag)" also had a great impact. I'm very fond of "Just for One Day" because it's an upbeat, lighthearted song, a counterweight to what sometimes felt like a lot of sadness. "I Burned Your Picture (Jag brände din bild)" is another favorite. The lyrics are beautiful: "*I burned your picture/ with loss as fuel/ and the flame was blue . . .*" Very dramatic and lovely.

I wrote the lyrics for "Coffee and Tears (Kaffe och tårar)" with a good friend of mine in mind who'd committed suicide. The man he loved had left him, and he didn't want to live anymore. It was awful. I'll never forget that funeral. There were only young people inside the church.

Later in my solo career, a big step was writing "Sparrow-Eye." It was the first song that was entirely my own. Anders Herrlin was my producer, and it was our first collaboration. I had an offer to write film music for a television series by the same name. The title spoke to me and sparked the song. The television series came out in 1989, and the song became extremely popular. It meant a lot to me and many others, I later came to understand.

I also performed at many charity events during these years. One of the early ones was at Cirkus, and many big names participated. [European celebrities] Carola, Lill-Babs, Arja Saijonmaa. The king and queen sat in the audience, and everything was recorded for television.

I was anxious and kept singing the "sixth" wave instead of the "seventh" wave. I was also supposed to sing "Toward Unknown Seas" and play the piano. They'd set up a microphone for me, but it started to slide downward, and I tried to lean toward it as best I could. Guitarist Lasse Wellander stepped in and tried to hold the mic for me out of the picture. Lactic acid built up in his arm toward the song's end, and the whole mic trembled. It was distressing, but no one saw it, not on TV, anyway. It turned out all right in the end.

I slowly discovered myself and took more control over how I expressed myself musically. I was less wishy-washy and could finally communicate what was right for me. Still, there's a standing joke about me, where they imitate me and say, "This was great!" And after a pause, " . . . or?"

CHAPTER 7

In the kitchen in Djursholm in January, 2015.

Moving up in the world.

———————

"**A**nd do you remember, Marie, when [Swedish Prime Minister] Olof Palme was murdered?"

Marie Dimberg is with us in Djursholm today. She has a stack of photos that Marie is expected to sign. We're in the kitchen, Marie Dimberg, Micke, Marie, and I. Marie slowly signs her autograph with a silver pen while Micke makes coffee. The cat Sessan rubs her head against the chair legs.

"Yes, it was awful," says Marie as she continues to write carefully. "I admired Olof Palme and looked up to him. My whole family adored him."

Marie Dimberg leans back in her chair and recalls the incident. It was the same evening the *The Seventh Wave* tour opened in Halmstad. The concert was a success, and they were about to start the after-party when rumors started flying.

"This was before mobile phones and the internet," she reminds us. "I called TT [news agency] repeatedly to find out what had happened. Per and Åsa were there to celebrate the tour premiere with us. In the end, we got confirmation that he was indeed murdered. We sank to the floor in the hotel hallway and sat there. We didn't even go down to the bar. Everything just stopped."

Marie nods. She remembers, too. "Yes, it was a shock," she says. "I was in complete disbelief. My family admired the Social Democrats and Olof Palme. Father often talked about how great it was that the

Social Democrats were in power in Sweden and instilled a sense of respect for them."

"Do you remember when you sang for Palme?" asks Marie Dimberg.

"Yes, how could I ever forget that?"

On the same day that Olof Palme was to be buried, Marie was asked to sing Ulf Schagerström's "Toward Unknown Seas" on *Rapport's* morning broadcast [a Swedish news program]. It was recorded in Gothenburg, and Fredrik Belfrage was the host.

"You performed at KB in Malmö the night before," says Marie Dimberg. "I drove you to Gothenburg during the night. You rested during the drive to be fresh and ready to perform. I asked my sister to join us so I wouldn't fall asleep at the wheel. It was the first and only time I've run over an animal so far. It was a rabbit. You felt the bump when the car hit it, but I didn't want to upset you, so I said we'd run over a rock."

"What? You've never told me that!"

"Yup, that's what happened. And hopefully, it won't ever happen again. So scary."

They arrived on time for the TV morning broadcast, and Marie sang "Toward Unknown Seas" to her idol while playing a grand piano.

"I struggled not to cry the whole time," says Marie. "But I'm glad I got a chance to honor him."

When Roxette started touring, Marie Dimberg remembers, politics was a constant topic of discussion. Marie Fredriksson came in from the left wing, while Per was more conservative. It could get quite heated during long nights at the bar, with Marie Dimberg agreeing with Marie on one topic and Per on another.

"You never really agreed, Per and you," she says. "You've never done that."

It was a great honor for Marie to sing on the day of Olof Palme's funeral, and Marie Dimberg points out that it was also then that respect grew for Marie, and she began to stand out among other Swedish artists.

"You moved to another level then, same as when you participated in the big, televised charity gala at Cirkus the same year. You were finally thought of as an artist to the Swedish people. And with the album *The Seventh Wave,* the people embraced you. Your music represented something more profound than chart placements on [Swedish radio show] *Svensktoppen.*"

With a few solo albums under her belt, Marie was one of Sweden's most beloved artists. Two years later came "It Must Have Been Love," and the whole world knew who Marie Fredriksson and Roxette were.

"You usually talk about being a twin, Marie," says Marie Dimberg. "That you have strong opposites in you. And that applies to your voice as well. Strong and fragile, Swedish and English, comforting and challenging, powerful and vulnerable. I think that's what made the whole world listen to you."

But at first, it was the Swedish Marie who dominated. "You were so much bigger in Sweden than Roxette was initially," says Marie Dimberg. "In retrospect, I wonder how we managed everything."

In 1988 came the double album *The Flying Dutchman (Den flygande holländaren)* with Swedish artists who interpreted [Swedish folk singer] Cornelis Vreeswijk.

"You made a fantastic effort together with Eldkvarn on the song 'Some People Walk in Tattered Shoes (Somliga går med trasiga skor),'" says Marie Dimberg. "You stepped into the studio and knew exactly what to do. It was magical. You also received a Grammi [Swedish Grammy] that year for your Swedish singing efforts, not for Roxette."

Marie Dimberg accepts the stack of freshly signed photos and tucks them into her bag. "You always do your thing without a doubt," she continues. "Like when you were a part of Artists Against Nazis (music gala) in 2001 and did 'For Those Who Love (För dom som älskar),' do you remember that?"

"Yes, Bo Kaspers was the house band, and there were so many difficulties surrounding them. So I thought, what the heck, I'll do it myself."

"Exactly, I remember it so clearly. It was at the Globe [now named the Avicii Arena], and you did the song alone on a piano. It was so powerful. I still get shivers just thinking about it."

Marie Dimberg praises Marie Fredriksson's fierce performances and how when it's time to deliver, she doesn't hold back. "And that's still the case," she says. "Remember the inauguration of the City Tunnel (railway link) in December 2010 in Malmö? Several artists were supposed to participate, including you. I'd made sure it wouldn't be too cold. I know how you hate to be cold. They said they would have heating fans, but no. It's freezing when we get there, and you had technical difficulties. But you powered through, and you performed so incredibly well."

"Think of all the photos I've signed," says Marie. "Oh Lord, many thousands! And think of all the times we've said, 'Hi, I'm Marie . . . and I'm Per . . . and we are . . . Roxette!' on different radio channels. We rambled that in our sleep. Nowadays, we only do that when it's for something special. We're not trying to be difficult; sometimes, you just don't want to.

"The years have gone by. Some of the pop star gestures feel outdated and a bit silly. As if we've outgrown them. Roxette has been around for almost thirty years. It can feel awkward doing the same things you did when you were much younger. So, some things you still have to do as a treat, while some other things are a bit dated."

CHAPTER 8

"Nobody recognized me."

Marie's story about the disease.

———————

Until July 2003, Micke thought I seemed more or less like myself, despite the disease. But during the summer, something changed. We were on our way to Halmstad from our summer house in Haverdal. Micke asked me to close the door behind me. I couldn't figure out what he meant. I couldn't make sense of it. What did he want me to do?

Later in the day, we were serving hot dogs to the kids. I took one and squirted mustard and ketchup on it before placing the hot dog into the bread. It was as if I'd forgotten in what order it usually went.

That evening, I couldn't set the table properly. I walked around with various cutlery in my hand without understanding where to place them. Logical household chores that I've done a thousand times and could probably do in my sleep became indecipherable puzzles.

This was six months after the so-called Gamma Knife surgery operation.

We consulted with the oncology department at Karolinska Hospital and then went home. While Micke drove the car home, the children and I took a plane. We preordered a taxi to pick up the kids and me at the airport. I couldn't tell the taxi driver where we lived. The knowledge was utterly gone. Somehow we made it home. The children helped explain, and the taxi company tracked down the address. That's how bad it was. And I don't even remember this incident. Micke told me about it.

Micke called my doctor, who said it was common after the type of radiation I'd been exposed to for some swelling in the brain. That swelling hit my logic center. When Micke said, "look there," and pointed, I'd look at his finger. If he asked me to go to the basement and grab a bottle of wine and a CD, it was too many steps to remember in my mind. The basement, wine, and the CD. I couldn't fit them together. It wasn't possible.

I took a lot of cortisone to reduce the swelling in my brain after the Gamma Knife procedure. The maximum allowed dosage was thirty-two tablets a day. Micke's mother had to help me remember all the pills. I swelled up in my face so much that I looked like a completely different person. Everyone used to know my face, but now nobody recognized me.

It wasn't that I needed to be recognized, but that no one recognized me as myself. For who I was, in what used to be my life. Every time I looked in the mirror, I was shocked.

Suddenly it became so quiet. Fewer and fewer called. I felt so awfully lonely. I was used to being in the center of events, and now I was relegated to the periphery. Many friends disappeared during the illness. They were uncomfortable, especially when I swelled up and looked so different.

But there were exceptions.

My best friend Pähr Larsson was always by my side. He cared about how I was doing, and he treated me the same, no matter how bloated I was. For that, I am eternally grateful to him.

Once, we went out and had lunch at a restaurant. When we met mutual friends, they only talked to Pähr. They didn't recognize me. It was hard. It felt like I no longer existed.

The same thing happened when Per and I were at a restaurant in Halmstad. People came up and asked him for an autograph but didn't see me. Or rather, they didn't realize that I was me.

We went to Miami Beach on vacation with the Gessle family and the Öfwerman family during this time. I sat by the pool, alone and swollen, feeling disgustingly ugly and unable to participate in what the others were doing or talking about. I didn't understand what I was thinking. How could I possibly have agreed to this trip? *What the hell am I doing here?*

Everyone felt sorry for me, but it was like no one had the strength to spend time with me. There was too much sadness and misery surrounding the situation. I don't think I've ever felt so alone. Clarence's wife, Marika, came up and kindly spoke to me sometimes, which was nice. But I felt friendless. Nobody wanted to be around me simply because it wasn't fun. It was too hard.

And concerning Micke — I always wanted to look nice for my partner, not as drastically different as I did. I never mentioned it to Micke, but I thought I might have to get a divorce. I had no zest for life, and I didn't think things would work out for the better. I wasn't necessarily thinking about death; I just felt so ugly and hated the cortisone.

Of course, I didn't really want to get a divorce. I was simply afraid that Micke would leave me because I looked so damn horrible. And it could be hard to connect with him at times. He had his grief and worries to bear, and often there was too much pain in the way for us to find closeness.

Shortly after Miami, when back home in Sweden, something else happened that devastated me. We'd been to Danderyd Hospital because my fingers and leg had swollen from all the medication — fifty tablets of various kinds, according to particular schedules.

When my fingers swelled up, my rings cut into my flesh. It happened so dramatically fast. We left in a hurry, picked up Oscar from school, and went directly to a goldsmith to get help to saw off the rings, the wedding ring that I got from Micke. Our ring. A goldsmith had to saw and cut it off, or else the next step would've been to cut off my finger.

I kept the pieces, and when we celebrated our twentieth anniversary, Micke surprised me with new rings. But still. It was traumatic, as if the time Micke and I had left together had been symbolically severed.

I also have another strong memory from this time. Micke and I were invited for dinner and a show by a couple of friends. There were many guests. After dinner, [magician] Joe Labero wanted help from someone in the audience for a magic trick. He pointed at me and asked, "You there, in the white suit, could you come up here?"

I went up to him, and he asked the audience for some applause. He told me to hold a card. When I did, he asked me my name. I said, "Marie," and he was astonished. He recognized my voice and realized it was me. It was as if someone had poured ice-cold water over him.

I completely lost my identity. I *became* cancer. That was all I was, and I hated every second of it. I was overwhelmed with loneliness, and at the same time, I didn't want to see anyone. Nothing added up, and I was torn between those extremes.

Sometimes I had to force myself to go out. It felt like I would die inside if I didn't. That I wouldn't survive mentally. Marika and Åsa had lunch with me sometimes. But my God, how people stared. I remember once snapping at an old lady, "Please stop staring; I'm not dead yet."

At this time, I remembered that my ID card had expired. I panicked. I simply *had to have* an ID card, another symbolic object. Inger drove me into town to take a picture for the card. Strangely, it was as if I'd forgotten what I looked like. I imagined that the ID card would somehow show the 'real' me. But when I saw the picture, I didn't want the card anymore. I didn't want it to prove who I was. Or rather, I couldn't stand the fact that the person in the picture *was* me.

When we finished the album *The Change*, we needed an image for the cover. I didn't want to show my swollen face. Micke suggested that I draw a self-portrait instead. So I did, and I also made portraits of some friends. Creating art again felt so fun and inspiring, like a quiet freedom to sit at home and draw. If there was anything positive that came out of the swelling in my face, it was that I found my way back to painting and drawing. I loved it. I really enjoyed riding in a taxi into Decorima and taking my time to choose paper and materials. I've had two art exhibitions in Stockholm and one in Gothenburg, and I sold out of everything. When all the tours are over, I'll continue with my art. I can't wait to sit with paper and crayons again.

Eventually, I secretly stopped taking the cortisone without understanding how serious it was to do so. But I hated it so much. I was also careless with the epilepsy medicine. I lived in a kind of denial, in another world where I didn't have to take medication. This led to several epileptic seizures. I don't remember much about them, but Micke told me about them.

One time we were up on the top of Mullfjället [mountain] in Duved with Clarence's family to have a picnic. We'd brought grilled chicken and a bottle of wine. I'd worried all the way up the lift, and maybe it was that fear that started a seizure that was about to occur. I was thinking to myself, *why on earth would we go up here*, as I was scared and hated it . . . and I hadn't taken my epilepsy medicine.

Before the attack, Micke noticed that he couldn't converse with me properly. He asked if I remembered my date of birth. "Yes, that's good," I replied. Whatever he asked, I answered the same thing.

"Yes, that's good."

"What's your name?"

"Yes, that's good."

How scary for Micke. He thought I had a new brain tumor. He tried to get an ambulance helicopter there, but it wasn't possible. Finally, two ambulance skiers arrived with a sled.

Once we were sledding down the mountain, I woke up and thought it was splendid. I heard the whistling of the skis and saw all the sparkling snow and a bright blue sky. Like a beautiful dream. A magical moment. It's still a positive memory for me.

But it was awful for both Micke and the kids. They were frightened. I've had seizures like that four times so far. Stress and swelling in the brain can have that effect. Micke immediately notices if I become absent. Once when we were having dinner for Marie and Tomas Ledin, he noticed that I wasn't there and called for an ambulance.

When the ambulance arrived, I sat in my armchair, utterly calm. They asked how I was, and I said it was fine. The ambulance driver turned to Micke and asked why he'd called, as I seemed to be perfectly okay. But when they asked for my date of birth, and I replied, "it's fine," they understood. I had to go to the hospital and was there for two days.

One might think that it was irresponsible of me to stop taking the cortisone. It sounds vain. But I became a different person. Someone who I saw as ugly and disgusting, who acted like someone else. I lost all hope and life force. Finally, I started to take a turn for the better shortly after returning home from the horrible trip to Miami. Micke said to me, "It's all going to turn out all right."

His conviction aroused such strength in me. I believed him. I felt revived by a sudden rebellion: *Just you wait, you bastards. I'm gonna show you!* I'd hit rock bottom but decided it was fucking enough now.

I want to urge people with this book to take care of one another. I know what it feels like when other people turn their backs on you. Try to give a bit of hope to someone who has lost their way. Help them understand that they will turn a corner and that life can improve again.

CHAPTER 9

"Almost nobody believed in Roxette."

In Marie's words.

———————

Per and I were different in many ways, but we still shared a deep love for pop music, loving a lot of the same bands, such as the Monkees and the Beatles. Sometimes we talked about the possibility of working together, but we weren't initially serious about it.

In the early eighties, Tom Petty, who was Per's big idol, released a song with Stevie Nicks from Fleetwood Mac, "Stop Draggin' My Heart Around." It inspired us to talk a little more seriously about singing and playing together. We initially did two songs together, "Nobody Can Like You (Ingen kan som du)" and "Before You Go, Come Back (Innan du går, kom tillbaka)." We worked at breakneck speed, writing both songs at Per's home one evening. We composed the music together, and Per wrote the lyrics. In summer 1985, we went on a minor tour with acoustic guitars and sang the vocals as harmonies. In addition to Per and me, Mats "MP" Persson and Lasse Lindbom were with us. We called ourselves the Exciting Cheeses. The name came about because Lasse had been inside a grocery store when we were trying to decide what to call ourselves and saw a sign for "Exciting Cheeses."

Rolf Nygrens, CEO of EMI, thought that we should try recording songs in English together. Almost nobody else thought I should join forces with Per, as his popularity had declined while mine was on the upswing. That was the prevalent view. Gyllene Tider broke up when Anders Herrlin dropped out, and Per's solo career wasn't going well. On the other hand, I was having success with my solo records.

Lasse was against the idea. He wanted to make a record with me in America. He and I were already talking about aiming abroad before any talk of me collaborating with Per. Lasse used to say, "You sing as well as Aretha Franklin."

Kjell at EMI was also against it. He liked my Swedish material so much. He thought that I could record English songs with Per as a side project but that it was Sweden that I should target.

Overall, a lot of people were skeptical. Some mentioned that I was the voice of the Swedish spirit, so why was I going to make English pop music with someone who had already peaked?

But I never hesitated. I was sure about it. Most of all, the United States was alluring to me. I'd never been, and Per and I dreamed of playing there. We had our friendship that we built up over several years, and we wanted to go out into the world.

Roxette's name comes from a song title by [English pub rock band] Dr. Feelgood. Per had thought Gyllene Tider would use the name abroad.

But it became ours.

The first song Roxette recorded was called "Neverending Love." Already back then, Clarence was hired as a producer and has been involved ever since. The rest of the band was initially Werner Modiggårdh on drums, Tommy Cassemar on bass, Mats "MP" Persson on guitar, and Clarence on keyboard.

Per had originally made "Neverending Love" in Swedish for Pernilla Wahlgren. Then it was called "Black Glass (Svarta Glas)." But she didn't like it.

Rolf suggested using two singers for the song and singing it in English. I didn't think the song was very good, and was far too poppy for my taste. But I gave it a chance. It quickly became a summer hit in Sweden in 1986, but wasn't as successful abroad.

We struggled to make it big and waited anxiously for something to happen. We said yes to everything and everyone overseas who showed even the slightest interest.

Then there were some twists and turns.

A German TV show called *Pink* received a cancellation, and we jumped on board with two days' notice. They booked Status Quo and us, and the program wanted each to perform in different 'workplaces.' We were to perform at a hospital and dance with the patients, which wasn't easy because one was in an orthopedic cast, and another was in a wheelchair.

It's too bad there's not a recording of this, as the whole setup sounds so far-fetched that you need evidence to prove it happened. Richard Parfitt and Francis Rossi from Status Quo danced with the nurses. Per and I rolled in on a hospital bed. We sat in our stage costumes in the middle of the patients and doctors. When the bed was pushed into the room, we jumped off it and started singing "Neverending Love." Absolutely surreal.

We did so much playback the first few years. I don't know how often we found ourselves lip-syncing in strange outfits. We had the ugliest stage clothes in the world. When we recorded the video for "Neverending Love," I had a black dress made of artificial leather. It had a wasp waist and a long triangle at the back, making me look like an insect. I dyed my hair copper red and cut it into a bob. It didn't look that great, but these were my first attempts to find a new style. I wanted to break off from my Swedish look, which was much more sweet and bohemian. But fucking hell, we looked like crap.

Right from the beginning, we had our different roles in Roxette. I was more laid-back, bluesy, and jazzy, while Per's appearance was more pop-ish and upbeat. The mix of the two of us was unique. I think our differences are part of Roxette's success. We created something exceptional together, Per and I.

We thought that we would write the songs together as well. But we soon gave up on that. No one can compete with Per in terms of productivity and pace. Per wrote fast, and he wrote in English, which I wasn't used to. So I focused on fronting the band, taking center stage, and he wrote most of the songs. I was fine as long as Roxette didn't have the same sound as Gyllene Tider. I didn't want us to make the same kind of light pop songs that they did. So there was some give and take, but our best sides came forth when we were together. We were a force to be reckoned with.

Roxette's first album is called *Pearls of Passion*. There is a song on it called "Soul Deep." It felt like Per wrote it for me. With that song, something clicked. It showcased my skills. He began writing songs to match my vocal style, using my voice as an instrument. He knew what notes blended well and how to bring out and use my vocals. It felt great to finally be singing in a deeper, well-rounded way.

When you see the video for "Soul Deep," it's clear I let loose. Oh my God. And the high heels I wore! And I also wore a short dress. It looks crazy! I danced around in sky-high heels and gave it my all. Anne-Lie Rydé, Petra Nielsen, and Efva sang backup. Rewatching that video, I saw how much I longed to own it and how badly I wanted to stake my claim. I was tired of the Swedish wussiness. I was always expected to stand in front of some sort of ocean backdrop and look so delicate.

Marie Dimberg told me afterward that she knew back then that something big was about to happen. The part of me that loved acting and being onstage was coming out. I felt alive being theatrical, and finally was able to show my strengths. It will sound arrogant to say this, but at that moment I sensed that I could really cross over internationally. It wasn't a belief I shared out loud, since nobody would probably understand where I was coming from. Not even Per, although he knew I had the desire and energy for it.

Something within me was simply dying to come out. A whirlwind of emotions that craved a creative outlet. I wanted to do everything at once. My transformation with Roxette onstage came entirely from within. I exploded and was all over the stage, jumping, dancing.

***

That said, internationally, *Pearls of Passion* didn't take off. But we had to start somewhere.

While I was making my third solo album, *After the Storm*, Per wrote the songs for Roxette's second album. If "Neverending Love" hadn't become a big hit in Sweden, Roxette might not have been allowed to make another album, and our collaboration would've ended.

Things were happening on two fronts now.

I have no idea how I managed everything in those years. My Swedish career was at a high point when I started with Roxette. *After the Storm* sold 250,000 copies. And Kjell at EMI, as I said, didn't think I should split my focus. There was some tension about where to put my energy. But deep down, I knew where I wanted to put my focus. Making it big abroad with Roxette was my dream. We printed T-shirts that said *Today Sweden — Tomorrow the World!* Everyone laughed at us, but he who laughs last laughs the loudest.

Everything happened quickly. We went on the tour Rock Around the Kingdom in 1987 with Eva Dahlgren, Orup, and Ratata. Marie invited record label executives from Germany, Italy, and Belgium. Doors began to open.

Anders Herrlin [engineer/programmer] came in and helped us find what became Roxette's sound. After our first single, Clarence wanted to bring in his band of musicians. Staffan played guitar initially, then Jonas Isacsson became the band's guitarist, while Tommy Cassemar continued to play bass. Pelle Alsing played drums and has been in the band ever since.

When Per presented "The Look," Clarence and I agreed that it was the edgiest song Per had written. It was an exciting new track. When we recorded it, guitarist Jonas was goofing around in the studio, imitating a stanza from the Beatles song "I Want to Tell You." Clarence heard it and asked him to do it again. It became a part of the song and the intro to "The Look."

When Per presented the song "Dangerous" to me, I wasn't enthused. I probably thought it was a little too tepid or sugary. I was skeptical when Per wanted to take it on the Rock around the Kingdom tour. But now, in retrospect, it is one of my favorites.

When the album *Look Sharp!* came out in October 1988, Per filmed Clarence and I promising to shave our heads if it didn't sell more than 170,000 copies in Sweden before Christmas, which was what *Pearls of Passion* had sold in two years.

It took three weeks. We got to keep our hair.

Look Sharp! was our second album and quickly became a bestseller here at home.

I experimented more with my style. When Mattias Edwall was going to take pictures of me for the cover of the single "It Must Have Been Love," I cut my hair short and dyed it blond. I instantly knew it was the right look for me. I also adopted more of a rock style with my outfits. I felt at home in leather jackets, leather pants, and stylish boots.

Our dream of breaking through in the US took some time. The US arm of our record company rejected "The Look" because they felt an American radio station would never play a song from a Swedish group.

We broke in the US thanks to Dean Cushman, an American exchange student in Borås who brought the album *Look Sharp!* back to the states. He liked it so much that he sent it to his hometown radio station in Minneapolis, Minnesota. They had a program where listeners could request to hear their favorite albums. It gathered dust there until Dean decided he wanted his record back. The radio DJ was curious why the album meant so much to Dean and played the first song on air, "The Look." And the rest is history. Radio station after radio station started playing it. Per's peculiar lyrics were heard across the American continent:

One, two, three, four
Walking like a man
Hitting like a hammer
She's a juvenile scam
Never was a quitter
Tasty like a raindrop
She's got the look
Heavenly bound
Cause heaven's got a number
When she's spinning me around
Kissing is a color
Her loving is a wild dog
She's got the look . . .

It's completely crazy and wonderfully lyrical. Per wrote the song by jotting down the first words that came to mind, whatever suited the rhythm so he'd have something to sing while composing. He thought he'd eventually rewrite the verses but keep the chorus where I sing *she's got the look*. Per thought the nonsense lyrics sounded so cool that he wanted to keep them. I thought it suited him much better, so he kept it.

And then it began to climb the charts.

I'll never forget when "The Look" went straight up to fiftieth place on the *Billboard* charts in the US. To be included on an American music chart was amazing! When "The Look" hit number one in the US, Per was at home in Halmstad, and I was in Stockholm. I celebrated at Café Opera with, among others, [Blue Swede lead vocalist] Björn Skifs, who had hit number one in the US with "Hooked on a Feeling."

We suddenly got the chance to go to New York to record the video for "The Look," and I barely even had a passport. Director Peter Heath wanted to make Per and me look like international stars in the video. I got the most attention because at the end I sit on a toilet and sing — fully dressed and with the lid down — but it was considered shocking at the time. In the English press they wrote the headline, *She's Got the Loo.*

Since I loved to put on a show, it was a complete dream to record music videos. We've worked with such fantastic directors and made some unbelievable shoots.

It rolled on. We hit number one in the US four times. Absolutely incredible. Who would even dare to dream of something like that?

Our second number one came in 1989 with "Listen to Your Heart." Per wrote it after talking to a friend who had marital problems, and the song was the advice he gave his friend. The video was recorded in the ruins of Borgholm [Sweden]. The Americans wanted us to film there. They filmed from a helicopter as we played onstage in front of a large audience who were handed sparklers to hold in their hands. I wore a short black dress and was barefoot. It ended up with a very atmospheric vibe.

Our third US number one was "It Must Have Been Love." We originally recorded it as a Christmas song in 1987 as "It Must Have Been Love (Christmas for the Broken Hearted)." Later, Touchstone Films asked Per if he could write a song for a movie they were working on. It was an unassuming boy-meets-girl story with Richard Gere and a relatively unknown Julia Roberts. Per didn't think he had time to write anything new, so sent the Christmas single. Director Garry Marshall liked it. But we had to alter the lyrics to fit the film better. It didn't work as a Christmas song. The plot in the movie was also slightly changed to suit the song. "It Must Have Been Love" became the theme song for *Pretty Woman*. We had no idea that the film would become one of the most-watched films in the world.

"Joyride" was our fourth number one in the US. The chorus line *"Hello, you fool, I love you"* came to Per when Åsa had left a note for him at home on the kitchen table with the same lines. We recorded the video for it in a desert outside of Los Angeles. Per and I sat in a red Ferrari and played guitar. I mainly remember that it was terribly hot and that the Americans we worked with were compltely professional.

Even though our songs are well-known in the US, we were never as famous there as the rest of the world. It's a bit disappointing. Otherwise, Roxette's success exploded around the globe. Songs like "The Look" and "Joyride" were simultaneously number one in twenty-six countries.

Money began to flow in, and I bought a maisonette apartment on Västmannagatan. A charming two-bedroom apartment with a living room, kitchen, and balcony. It was my first apartment, and I got to furnish it myself. I'd always dreamed of having a grand piano, and I wanted to buy one, whatever the cost. The dream came true when I lived in Vasastan. The grand piano I purchased was a Bösendorfer. I'll never forget when they brought it home. I mean, it took four people to carry it.

I'm still so happy about the grand piano. I often think of what it means to me as I sit by it at home. The whole family enjoys sitting at it and playing.

My pride over becoming a pop star was enormous, that being an international singer actually turned out to be my career. I'd hardly dared to believe such a possibility when I was child, and after Roxette became famous there were moments when it was completely unreal. Per and I'd look into each other's eyes onstage and have this breathtaking sensation. "Now we are big," he'd say. And I could only agree. Yes, now we've made it. Now we're a big deal.

What we got to experience as Roxette is indescribable. It was a victory parade without comparison — enormous, crowded arenas in country after country. Germany, Holland, Australia, Russia . . . we toured over forty different countries around the world.

I loved coming up with theatrical effects for the stage. On the *Look Sharp!* tour, I appeared onstage in a black half-length wig. After a song, I tore it off to reveal my usual short and blond self. It always caused such an uproar! This was before the internet, so everyone was equally surprised every time.

The *Joyride* tour was even more massive. The hysteria was turned up another notch. It's extraordinary when fame happens as suddenly as it did for us. All at once, I'm an international artist, yet I'm still the same person. It was a magical time. I was flashy and exuberant, taking over the entire stage everywhere we went. Many thought that I was individually Roxette — that it was my stage name. I'd somehow managed to become the center of attention.

I've never had stage fright. I've been afraid of many things, but never of singing and standing on a stage. It was as if I'd been waiting to let loose in a large arena. I don't know where all that power had been hiding. As a Swedish artist, I was more introverted and thoughtful. But in Roxette? Oh my God!

When I stood on the stage, I felt centered and self-assured. Oscar recently found old clips that I hadn't seen in many years, where I put on one heck of a show, stirring up the audience as I ran back and forth.

Roxette is a feel-good band. We're not enmeshed in scandal. The audience seems to get in a good mood when they see us. We've always wanted to convey an upbeat intensity. That's the message behind what we do: positive energy.

Some criticized us for playing in places like China. But we've always maintained that we're apolitical and play for all people. We spread warmth and joy. It felt like we were doing something important for the people and their culture. And nothing but love and joy was reciprocated.

Someone hung up a banner in the concert hall that said, "One World, One Unity," and it became political. The authorities also wanted to censor the phrase "making love" [from "Sleeping in My Car"]. But I kept it in, and nobody noticed. From the Western world, I think it was only Wham! that had played in China up to that point, while bands like the Rolling Stones and other popular bands had been turned down.

———

No one in the band has set about to be difficult or cause problems. We've wanted to set a good example. But one time, I decided to act like a 'pop star.' It was in Zurich. I stayed on the top floor of a nice luxury hotel. Pähr was visiting. We couldn't be bothered to go out to eat and ordered room service instead. The plates with our food had large metal lids over them. And suddenly, I felt mischievous.

"Now I'll show them who's a rock star," I said to Pähr and opened the window. First, I looked closely to make sure no one was standing below. Then I threw out the silver lids, and they made a terrible clattering as they hit the stone pavement outside. It was oddly liberating. *I did it! I did it!*

Pähr said, "That's right, Marie, show 'em who's in charge." We laughed all evening.

As the artist Marie Fredriksson in Roxette, I could be a bit cocky. I wasn't afraid of anyone. My attitude was, *don't push me around.* Maybe something from my childhood brought those feelings up. There were times when I pushed the boundaries. When Micke and I had met, we were going to take Air France from Paris to São Paulo. This was the period when I walked around in leather pants and sunglasses and signed autograph after autograph at airports. Something went wrong with the ticket machine when we got our boarding passes. We were in first class. Micke ended up not sitting next to me, and instead, there was a stranger I didn't know.

The flight attendant told me to sit next to the man during takeoff, and we could change seats later. But I refused. I wanted to sit next to Micke, period, end of story. Finally, the pilot came down from the cockpit upstairs. He said he was commander-in-chief on the plane. I either had to sit or leave the plane.

Then I spoke the sentence, for the first and probably last time in my life: "Do you know who I am?"

He replied yes, he knew, but he had to take off from the airport regardless and that I needed to decide what to do, sit or get off the plane.

I was so in love and committed. I stood still and refused to move.

The tour leader Tor "Tosse" Nielsen solved the situation in three seconds by asking if the man next to me would change places. And he agreed, as simple as that.

Ugh, I'm so ashamed, thinking about that moment. But still — it was fun to challenge the boundaries occasionally. The flight attendants asked for autographs later on the trip.

The flights with Roxette have been quite dramatic at times. When we flew from Buenos Aires to Asunción in Paraguay, there was a terrible tropical rainstorm, complete with lightning and thunder. Everyone drank like crazy to quell the horror. Suddenly, lightning struck the plane, and everything went black. We finally managed to land, and the storm was thirty seconds behind us. It was as if the sky had opened. We entered the arrival hall, pale and drunk, where a large film crew waited. They held out a microphone to Per and me, asking us what we thought of Olof Palme.

It's not always easy to give fitting answers. At that time, we could barely talk at all. Another time, we flew from London to Tokyo and showed up dead tired. The press wanted to interview us at all costs, and the only question they wanted to ask was if we were a tree, what tree would we be? Per said Christmas tree, but I don't think I managed to answer.

———

It's a strange life, touring.

We went out for a year on the *Joyride* tour with only short breaks at home. We were basically locked in hotel rooms. I couldn't go out alone because of all the fans pushing and pulling on me, wanting different things. We had several bodyguards around us all the time. It was the same all over the world.

At home in Sweden, I lived by myself in my apartment. On tour, I longed for home, and when I got home, I longed to go on tour again. Onstage, everything was dandy. But once the tour was over, there was emptiness. It was offstage where life was hard.

It was dreadfully lonely, all that touring. When I was sitting in makeup after a gig, I'd often break down and cry out of fatigue, loneliness, and feeling lost. Per had met Åsa early in life, and he had her with him when we were out and about. I had the rest of the band to hang out with, but I missed having someone to be close to. Music and love are so intertwined. I had a few relationships, but none worked out in the long run.

It got to me. I was onstage or in a studio, singing about love, but I didn't have it myself. The band could leave the stage and have privacy. Per and I couldn't. Notoriety was always with us, like a mask we couldn't take off.

Sometimes I'd call my mother, but it was difficult to talk about. She didn't understand what I was going through. She couldn't grasp it. And she wasn't particularly impressed, either. The *USA, so what,* she'd say, and tell me about a random happening in Östra Ljungby.

Tina was the one I usually called when I was alone in the hotel room with a glass of wine. The number of times that we must have talked on the phone, you can imagine the phone bills. But it meant so much to be able to connect with her.

Coming home to an empty, dusty apartment after touring was one of the most desolate experiences. It was impossible to unwind and relax. It also took a lot of energy, all that traveling. I started to get depressed. I'd want to hit the road again. In the end, it felt like there was no place in the whole world where I felt harmonious and at peace.

It was like there were two of me. One was the woman onstage with fantastic self-confidence and no fear. The other was the woman I was offstage, someone who constantly doubted herself. There's a difference between low self-confidence and low self-esteem. And in my career, I had a tremendous amount of self-confidence. I always knew I could sing. I loved the stage and could express myself there. I was comfortable in the role of performer.

But the person I was offstage was the opposite of the cocky artist. Before I met Micke, I felt lost and doubted myself. The more people who surrounded me on the tours, the lonelier I felt in the hotel room.

We drank a lot of alcohol when we were on tour. "Let's have a drink," everyone said. I drank way too much. There was stress, loneliness, partying, and big emotions all over the place. Had I not become ill, I might've become an alcoholic.

It was an extreme and sometimes excessive life, but my unhappiness wasn't about touring. Since childhood and Anna-Lisa's death, I'd carried my bad self-esteem with me. A pain festered in me that I couldn't bear, and I spent a lot of energy ignoring the wound. I had no interest in wallowing around in it. It was easier to say, "Woo-hoo, let's have a drink!" I didn't want to stop our momentum. I didn't dare stop.

We were exhausted from all the time changes and jet lag. And we barely had any spare time; that's how fast we were growing abroad. We traveled around so much that once I fell asleep during an interview in Japan.

Sometimes I'd invite friends along on tour. I'd miss all the social stuff happening at home, so it was cool to have someone with me for a while. Once Pähr visited me in Sydney and lived in my suite. One day we sat inside and relaxed and talked. Suddenly it started raining heavily, and without thinking, I said, "My God, I forgot to take my lawn furniture inside." Pähr still teases me that I thought about bringing in my furniture from the balcony at home in Sweden because it was raining in Sydney. I could get so out of it that I didn't know where home was.

Once I invited Efva to California. She'd just had a baby and wanted to get out of the house. I gave her the trip as a present for her fortieth birthday. Efva and I had a lot of fun, but she reminded me the other day of how I'd gotten angry at her one moment on the trip. We'd ordered breakfast in the room, and Efva complained that the bacon was burned. I snapped. By then, we had reached San Francisco. There we were, ordering a luxurious breakfast in a nice hotel, and she's bitching about a burned piece of bacon! But overall, it has always been fun to be able to invite friends along. It was a way to keep my private life going even though I was never home.

On the plus side, one of the best things about making as much money as I did was helping those I cared about, especially within the family. Mother got extra private help to deal with the effects of her Parkinson's disease. Some siblings got new teeth or temporary assistance when times were difficult. It meant a lot to me to have the means to help the family since we didn't grow up with much.

Shortly after I met Micke, Roxette went to South America. I was happy, newly in love, and touring life wasn't lonely anymore. I was rejuvenated. And the response we had from South America was spectacular. I was shocked by all the commotion when we arrived there. It gave me a wicked spurt of self-confidence, but it was also scary. People wanted too much. Fans banged on the car windows and wanted to touch us. We had several bodyguards, so we were safe, and Per and I downplayed all the fuss.

Do you know what the happiest moment is onstage? It's right when you take the first step into the arena and hear the audience's reaction. Imagine standing on a stage in São Paulo and shouting to 60,000 people, "Are you ready?"

And 60,000 people scream back, "YEAAAH!"

I get chills thinking about it. Our South American tour began on April 20, 1992, in Montevideo in front of 23,000 excited fans. Then, in Buenos Aires, we played in front of 50,000 people. And the next night in front of as many again. We had eleven concerts in South America that exceeded everyone's expectations.

At the same time, there was something frightening about Roxette's success. In Rio de Janeiro, 100,000 people showed up, and one person unfortunately died on the way to the arena. It felt like we had no control over the magnitude of our audiences.

Per and I had different attitudes about our success. He wanted to push forward and keep reaching for more. Per was more of a pop star than I was. He paid attention to chart placements and sales figures and thought it only natural to have lots of fans outside waiting for him after a show. He kept a fast pace. He never had any issues with being interviewed, whereas I thought interviewing was torture.

During these years, I received a lot of great offers for collaboration. Richard Marx, of "Right Here Waiting" fame, presented ideas several times. Peter Cetera from the band Chicago, who just had a solo hit with "Glory of Love," wondered if I wanted to sing a duet. But I declined. I didn't have the energy or time and didn't want to be away more than necessary. There was so much pressure in my life, and it wasn't possible to keep up with everything.

But when Frank Sinatra got in touch, I was not only highly flattered but also interested. He had plans for a duet record with several female artists. We were at our summer house in Haverdal at the time, and the postman delivered a package with a cassette with three different songs that I could choose from.

Josefin was just over a year old then. We played the songs in the living room, and "My Funny Valentine" really caught my interest. We went into the kitchen to fix breakfast and left Josefin in the living room. When we returned, we found her sitting in a sea of unraveled cassette tape. I'll never forget that sight. I would've liked to do the Sinatra project, but it never happened. He made a record with American female country singers instead.

There's one offer I regret not doing, though. Before the Olympics in Barcelona 1992, I was asked to sing a duet with Placido Domingo. In retrospect, I would've liked to have sung with him. But I was so stressed out. I knew what it would mean in terms of travel and effort, and I couldn't manage it all. Now I regret my decision.

Per and I were equally involved in Roxette's records up to *Joyride*. He, Clarence, Anders, and I were all there with opinions, fixing and testing everything. It was incredibly creative. But more and more, Per and Clarence took over. I had started a family, and at first, I thought Per didn't understand how having children might make someone want to slow down a bit. Per always wanted the next thing, to open another door.

Our fifth album *Crash! Boom! Bang!* came in 1994. It was recorded in Capri when Josefin was a baby. We added the song "Sleeping in My Car" at the last moment. Pelle was the only other one in the band who had children. Everyone was on me, pushing for a new tour. No one understood how I might have different priorities. Everyone thought we should go for it again.

Attitudes changed as more of the band had children. I was still looking forward to the tour once it was decided. I struggled to get in shape. I swam and ran. Then we did eighty-one concerts on four continents.

When Oscar was born in 1996, we took a break from Roxette. It was a relief to have some time off. I came out with my solo album *In a Time Like Ours* (*I en tid som vår*) and had a hit with the song "Faith (Tro)."

The break from Roxette lasted until 1998, when we recorded our sixth album, *Have a Nice Day*, in Marbella. From January to April, the whole gang lived together on a farm outside Marbella [Spain]. Many had their children and partners with them. Marika Erlandsson was there with her and Clarence's daughter Ella, who was just over a year old. Oscar was a little older.

We started collaborating with a new producer, Michael Ilbert. He'd previously worked with Gyllene Tider and Brainpool, an opening act for Roxette. Per thought Ilbert produced excellent guitar sounds. It was during the grunge era, so the sound was spreading to Roxette as well.

I ended up under Ilbert's thumb. He was strong-willed and only communicated with Per and Clarence. He'd push me around until I started crying. Ilbert said I had to sing songs repeatedly during the recordings, and Per and Clarence didn't notice that he was tearing me down. Nothing I did was good enough. I went from feeling safe and happy to losing all self-confidence.

It was Per, Clarence, and Ilbert. Three men and me. I felt more and more left out. The men decided, and no one cared what I thought. I lost my drive and ended up walking away. I wasn't very engaged when we recorded *Room Service*, which came out in 2001. There was one recording session where I was going to add vocals to the song "Milk and Toast and Honey." I took a taxi to the studio and had the taxi wait outside while I sang the song so that I didn't have to be there for a single second longer than I had to. That says something about the mood at the time.

It wasn't that Roxette didn't work out. We had different focuses at times. We were all so close, but sometimes we disagreed and needed our own space.

I was so pissed off when we recorded "Dressed for Success," for example. Per and Clarence ganged up on me and badgered me about my singing. I didn't get what they were looking for. I yelled at them to shut up and went into the studio, mad as a hornet. I nailed the song in one take.

Everyone agreed that it turned out great.

Per and I built Roxette piece by piece, and we had fun throughout. That's important to remember. Damn, how much fun we've had together! The best thing about Per is his sense of humor. But during that time, I was sick and tired of everything. When I look at my diaries from 2000 or 2001, it's clear how unhappy I was about the gigs. In Seattle in 2000, I wrote, "How long am I gonna be able to keep this up?" It felt like we'd hit a wall. Maybe the brain tumor was acting up as early as back then, but I didn't feel like doing anything involving Roxette.

Right before I got sick, Per and I agreed to take a break from the group. I called a meeting, and it was decided. Per seemed relieved. We both needed to get some space. The idea was that we would do Night of the Proms and then take time off. Night of the Proms was supposed to be a kind of finale.

But it never happened. Instead, I fell ill.

CHAPTER 10

Djursholm in January, 2015.

Images from the past.

The leg, the leg.

We're talking about Marie's leg as soon as we see each other. Her main concern about the upcoming tour in New Zealand and Australia again revolves around her foot and how it's twisting. The Botox injection helped with the Russian tour, but will it work again?

It's getting harder and harder for Marie to walk. She bears her burdens with her unique blend of grief and fighting spirit. Doubt and tears. Protruding chin, defiance, and hopefulness.

If only for the foot. It'd be fun to go on tour if she didn't have to deal with her foot cramping and twisting. But she's moving around with great difficulty, walking slowly and needing support along the way. She knows exactly where everything is at home, which makes movement easier.

Today we decided to pick photographs for the book. Marie and Micke are currently cleaning the room they use as an office. There are two large desks facing each other and bookshelves are along the walls. I stand and stare up at the shelves where [Swedish music awards] Rockbjörnen, Grammis [Swedish Grammys], MTV Awards, and various statuettes crowd together.

"Do you see all those awards? I have a whole storage unit full of gold records. It's impossible to display everything because there'd be nothing else on the walls. I was overjoyed every time we got a gold record, but it was too much sometimes. So many pictures have been taken of us shaking hands with a record company executive somewhere in the world," Marie says and then waves it off, quite literally. But then she turns around and smiles. "But you must know how appreciative I am. Make sure you share that. I'm happy and proud."

We rifle through the large boxes of Roxette photos, often coming across variations of what Marie has described, pictures of Marie and Per smiling happily with a gold record in their hands next to international record company representatives who also wear smiles. Marie is vague about where they were taken. Maybe in Germany. Or England. Sometimes she knows for sure; sometimes, the occasions get mixed up.

And that's certainly understandable.

It's easy to get lost among the pictures — box after box of stage photos, promotional shots, images from video recordings. We choose pictures that might work for the book and set them aside. It's both exciting and fun.

"Oh wow, this is a nice picture of you, Marie!"

"You look super cocky in this one!"

"What a cool jacket!"

"Wow, you're jumping so high!"

Marie smiles at my enthusiastic remarks, photo after photo. She looks pleased, but there's also a great deal of sadness in her eyes. Looking back on her past comes with strong, conflicting emotions. There's enormous joy and pride, of course. But also melancholy when she considers what she was able to do before. She misses the artist who bounded from one side of the stage to the other, firing up tens of thousands of screaming fans. Now she's not sure if she can stand throughout a concert.

"But do you know what makes me strong through this?" says Marie. "The fans. They've always been by my side. They're still here. Now they have families, but they still come to shows. They're so sweet. So friendly. Look here."

Marie walks to the desk where a framed list of the fans who started a world prayer chain when she became ill prominently stands. She wipes away her tears and points to another item; a Russian doll painted like her. She also picks out scrapbooks made from concert photos fans have sent to her. "I've received so many gifts over the years. A huge number of flowers, letters, and cards."

Fans also keep track of everything that has to do with Marie and Roxette. When I ask about the gap between her front teeth, when exactly it disappeared, Marie quips that she doesn't remember, but I can ask the fans. They know better than she does.

She swears that fixing the gap feels like something that happened a thousand years ago. She'd decided to fix it as soon as she could afford it and had the time. And sometime during the years with Roxette, it happened.

"The gap needed to go. It's as simple as that," she says. "Many tried to persuade me not to, claiming it to be charming, personal, and cute. But I've always hated it. I was teased for it when I was little. At school, they called me *gappy* (*gluggen*). That sticks with you. It was wonderful to remove it. I never regretted it, not for a second, no matter what people have said. Charming and personal, like hell it was. I'm glad it's gone."

Selecting images isn't an easy task. Not when there are so many. Several are from recordings of various music videos. There's one where Marie is sitting in bed while Jonas Åkerlund leans over the camera.

"Jonas has meant so much to Roxette and me. He's directed many of the videos we've made. That shoot was for 'I Wish I Could Fly.' I'm lying in a bed with black sheets and singing. He wanted to capture the feeling of waking up in the middle of the night when your imagination becomes distorted and strange. He's composed so many compelling images to create the right feeling."

I'm telling Marie about a Roxette fan who recently contacted me. Her name was Paula, and she was so sincerely happy that Marie wanted to tell the story of her life in a book since Marie has always cared so much about maintaining her family's privacy. Marie admits she's held back in interviews, partly because the discussions were never for her, she feels. And she felt awkward. Plus, the tabloids have been harsh with her.

"I had to hold back," says Marie. "When Roxette was at its high point, it could be too much."

Especially in vulnerable situations, it has felt detrimental to remain private, like when Josefin was barely two months old and had a respiratory virus infection. It was so severe that Marie and Micke had to stay in the hospital with her. "The door to our room had a glass pane, and we had to cover it because so many people were peeking in. Then, staff members started coming into the room to 'check' on us," she remembers. "They didn't mean any harm, but it was invasive, and in the end, we didn't know who was who or what they wanted."

Most expect privacy on airplanes, for example. Time feels suspended, and people want a bit of self-absorption. But there was no privacy for the band. And it wasn't just passengers, there were Roxette fans among flight crews, and it was common for flight attendants to ask for autographs. "It's not as frenzied as it used to be, but there were times back then when I felt trapped," says Marie.

[But still], "I'm above all so incredibly grateful for the fans. They mean so much. They are so loving, kind, and supportive."

I help Marie lift two large boxes crammed with pictures. We start to go through the first. They're primarily photos from the Roxette era. Then I find an odd one, someone lying across the floor dressed as Ronald McDonald. And standing above him are two record executives, Marie, Per — and Tina Turner!

Marie says it was a McDonald's campaign featuring Roxette, Tina Turner, and Elton John. Music downloading had just begun, and they wanted to market CDs. Fans could buy a CD for a reduced price from Roxette or one of the other artists for charity.

"One of the strange things that happened when Roxette became known worldwide," Marie continues, "is that we were suddenly among other stars. We were one of the gang. It was hard to grasp. Sometimes we had to pinch our arms, like when Tina Turner invited us home for dinner after the McDonald's spectacle.

"She had a fantastic home, and we had a great evening. She also thought my name was Roxette. She waved me over and said, 'Come here and sit with me, Roxette.' She ignored Per. We talked about exercise and moved on to Mick Jagger. Tina said it didn't matter how much running he did; he'd never escape himself."

Mick Jagger happens to be who Marie thinks was the coolest to have met. "We're sitting at the restaurant Sjömagasinet in Gothenburg. Micke and I and another couple were having dinner. Suddenly there's a tap on my back, and when I turn around, it's Mick Jagger standing there, saying he wants to say hello. From another table, Thomas Johansson waves and gives me a big smile, so I understand that he's the one who orchestrated it. I don't remember much of what I said. We mostly greeted each other. I told him I'd see them play in the evening, and he said, 'You should bring an umbrella.' And he was right because the rain poured down in Gothenburg! I was dying. I became like a little child. He was one of my idols who I grew up with!"

Mick was great, but Marie remembers something else as well. "He was so short! They were always so small, the big stars!"

Another time, says Marie, the family was on holiday in Thailand, and Ron Wood was in the same hotel. "He came over and said hello! He recognized me! He, a member of the Rolling Stones, said *I* was a famous artist that he liked. I almost fainted. It was both awesome and strange at the same time."

Among the photos of meeting other great artists and the photograph with Tina Turner, we also select an image of Marie with the Bee Gees and another with Elton John. The latter Marie met when he was in Stockholm at an event receiving the Polar Prize. "The press wanted a picture of us together. He was very nice, but I don't remember us talking about anything special," she says. "When Roxette was at its peak, we ran into one celebrity after another. But sometimes we couldn't greet all the people. It was too much. We were so tired and didn't know what to say."

It becomes a bit artificial and fake, says Marie. They'd shake hands and exchange courtesies, frantically looking for something more substantive to say — not just that they simply appreciated each other's music or that a particular song meant something to them.

Marie remembers one of her and Micke's first nights out together after Josefin was born. They planned an evening in town while

Micke's mother babysat. "It was a luxury to be together in town all by ourselves, as it is for all parents of young children."

They went to the cinema, ate at Café Opera, and decided to go to the Cadier Bar at the Grand Hôtel for one last beer. And through the large glass window, they see Thomas Johansson sitting with Elton John.

"By then, I was all tapped out," says Marie. "We wanted to stay in our private zone, without needing to interact or be polite, no matter how cool it would've been to chat [again] with such a great and fantastic artist."

We're looking through the boxes one one more time, selecting the most exciting photos, knowing we can exclude some later.

It ended up being quite a big pile before the day was over.

CHAPTER 11

"I thought I had hit the wall."

Marie's story about the disease.

Weren't there any symptoms of my tumor before the day I collapsed in the bathroom? Many people have asked, and I've pondered it myself. I know I felt depressed and didn't feel like myself. I lacked energy; I lacked joy. We'd been out touring a lot, and I wanted to be home with the kids. Something was bothering me, something didn't feel right, but I couldn't put my finger on it. I remember reading the book *The Law of Slowness* (*Långsamhetens lov*) by Owe Wikström, which was about slowing down to embrace the peace and seriousness of life instead of pushing ahead and forcing yourself to be so efficient all the time. I longed to be able to slow down. That's how it had felt for a year or so.

At the same time, we worked a lot and were on such a tight schedule that it was difficult to reflect too much on any oddities I noticed. We discussed putting Roxette on ice and eventually decided to take a break.

Micke also pointed out a few times before I got sick that I made strange association errors when we talked. I couldn't fully keep up with the conversation when someone referred to something that was said five minutes earlier. So, there were signs that were understood better in retrospect.

I mostly figured I was stressed, about to be burned out, and that notion depressed me. Sometimes I think it started my illness. Two years before the illness, I didn't feel well. I was worried about something but didn't know what it was. We traveled left and right until

I was completely exhausted. What if it was the stress that triggered the tumor to start growing?

Why me?

That's the question I ask over and over again. Micke said the other day that he came into the kitchen one morning, and I was sitting at the table in my bathrobe crying. I cried out, asking, "Why me?"

But then I changed my mindset and said, "Why *not* me?" Anyone can get a brain tumor, so why not me? I had it so incredibly well — a wonderful family, a fantastic career, significant wealth — so why should I be spared? It was as if I'd always known something like this could happen, a punishment for having it too good, quite simply.

It hasn't been easy for Micke and me to remain close during the illness; it's been tough to communicate in many ways. But music has always been a way for us to connect. We can reach each other through music, no matter how bad it's been.

There've been phases where we've done nothing but dwell on the disease. Eventually, we reach a point where we can no longer talk about it. The best thing to do then is work and get away from it for a while.

We've tried our best to keep the light and have hope. To not be prejudiced against alternative treatment, to be open-minded. Sometime in 2002, we tried a healing form called Reiki. A remarkable woman we knew named Anki came to our home and held her hands on different parts of my body to convey universal energy. Afterward, I'd feel much more relaxed and focused.

Anki knew a psychic, a unique individual. When he showed up at our house, he immediately drank a glass of Jägermeister and put on a CD to go into a trance. He switched to another album and drank another glass of Jägermeister. He started to speak in a different tone, an old-fashioned, solemn Swedish. He channeled the apostle John.

We sat there and listened, our mouths wide open. He talked about our lives as if we had a future. This was when we didn't think we had a future. When everything felt black, wherever we looked. We were starved of light. After the meeting, we were euphoric. We regained our faith that it could work out. That I had a chance to survive.

He envisioned us in a monastery, and our house in Spain looks a lot like a monastery. He talked about 'a heart,' and afterwards, for a long time, we tried to understand this reference. Pretty soon we figured it out. We usually call our house *El Corazón,* which means 'heart' in Spanish. That must be what he was referring to.

When he woke up from his trance, he was so drunk that he stumbled down from our attic, where we had had our meeting. We didn't know anything about this man. Maybe we were fooling ourselves. But it gave us hope. We absorbed everything that felt hopeful. It didn't matter what it was, as long as it gave us comfort and light in the endless darkness that surrounded us.

In August 2003, it was decided that I would have a third operation to remove the irradiated part of the brain. They also wanted to see if there were any living tumor cells left. After that operation, I sustained the more serious injuries I'm struggling with today. Post-operation, I suffered from aphasia. I knew what I wanted to say but couldn't verbalize the right words. I could hum, though, and singing without words was a great consolation.

But the words disappeared. It was infuriating.

For two years, I could barely say anything. Micke and I couldn't talk. I couldn't read, and I had no short-term memory. I lost everything I once knew. Lacking linguistics — that's hell. I couldn't speak, write, or express myself adequately.

Life became something completely different from what I was used to. I woke up and took a shower, then I would go into the office and sit down at the computer. But I couldn't use it. I became apathetic, sitting around for most of the day, looking out the window. Or even straight ahead. After a few hours, I ate and went to bed. That was the case for a few years. Total depression. Emptiness. Loneliness. Thank goodness for the children. Because of them, I had a reason to get myself together.

Micke could be uncompromising sometimes, and felt it was a matter of forcing myself to figure the proper wording out. He didn't fill in words for me or interpret what I meant. Others tried to help, but Micke believed that one learned faster by trying to express oneself. He was probably right, even if it was difficult sometimes.

You know what it's like when I talk to you [Helena]. Suddenly it stops. Names, days, whatever. Suddenly it's just gone. It can come back if I don't get stressed. But the conversation stops.

Thankfully, I can talk again. It's getting better and better. I'm elated when a new word comes, a word I haven't used in several years. It's the best. But some words are probably gone forever. For the album *Now!* I wrote a song, "The Last Waltz of the Summer." It felt like it took a hundred years to create!

Most things have improved, but some tasks are still complicated, like telling time. I know what time it is but can't say it. I mix up 'twenty to' and 'twenty past,' but usually, I know it, even if I can't articulate it. I've even made rhythms of the months to remember them in order: January, February, and now — March!

I'm unable to read books or magazines. I can't read the subtitles of a movie or use a computer. I used to love reading books, and always had one in progress. I miss that. I do watch a bit of TV, preferably the weather. I'm always checking it.

I can write a few words at a time. I have a calendar where I carefully write what I need to keep track of. But sometimes I have to repeat things to ensure I don't forget them. I've often written notes that I can't read afterward. I write too fast if I'm stressed and can't read it later. If I do too much at the same time, my mind locks up. The trick is to deal with everything at a leisurely pace. I've learned to write slowly and clearly. But I still get a lot wrong and can't spell well anymore.

I have a vision defect from the first operation, which I hate. One of my eyes sees nothing but a streak. I have to turn my head to the right to see where you are now, [Helena]. I know my home inside out, so that's not a problem. But somewhere like an airport, I wouldn't cope as well. If there will be crowds wherever I'm going, I need someone to accompany me.

At Erstagårdskliniken, I was given a rehabilitation plan to follow. They'd secretly helped Nelson Mandela with his rehabilitation, so it felt like a reliable and safe place to be. Micke drove me there every Sunday night, and I lived there during the weekdays. I got them to put in curtains, as I was so tired of looking out the windows.

My mental rehabilitation consisted of pointing at a green ball on a computer, even though it had the text "black ball" underneath. I was supposed to distinguish words from pictures, but I couldn't phrase them properly. However, the more that time went by, the worse that I felt, and my self-esteem plummeted. I felt hopeless, like an eternal patient.

Nine years after I became ill, my foot began to act up. It twists, which causes problems with my balance. I'm worried it will keep getting worse. And one of my legs has weakened, too. I have difficulty walking and am constantly afraid of falling. It is my greatest adversity to have lost my mobility in the way I have.

If you only knew how much I've fallen!

I love going out and walking. I walk with my trainer. As long as I can hold on to someone, I walk quite well. I need to keep using my frail leg; otherwise, it will worsen. I walk on our treadmill in the basement at home to improve leg strength. I considered a rehabilitation program with other people that had similar injuries. We checked it out, but I didn't want to do it. It was full of older people, and the thought of working out there depressed me.

Before I got sick, I was an active, mobile person. I danced and jumped around onstage. I trained in boxing and ran. I loved swimming, and still can in a pool in Spain. But here at home, people stare too much. I can't handle it. I'm an energetic person trapped in an injured body. It's so incredibly frustrating. It doesn't help to feel like when I go out, and people are staring, thinking, *How is she? What does she look like now?*

The leg and foot issues are hard to deal with, and unlike other symptoms, they've gotten worse. It feels like having my hands tied behind my back. I fall, get up again, fall. And I can't stand how much I have to depend on other people. During the hardest years, Micke has barely been able to leave me alone.

I've had a few friends. Pähr, who I told you about before, Clarence's partner Marika, and Åsa have stayed close. Pähr, in particular, was there for me, even though I sat and cried all the time. He started as a nurse and now heads the emergency room at Södersjukhuset, so he knows and understands what's going on. Pähr has enormous patience and makes me laugh in the middle of it all, even when I was bald and wearing a cap.

Ideally, I wanted to hide from people. But it was a survival thing. If I didn't go out and meet people, I would've died inside.

Micke's mother has been divine. Berit's helped us so much. She's cooked, comforted me, and helped me keep track of my medications. And she takes fantastic care of the children. The kids love their grandmother. Without her, we wouldn't have made it.

Sometimes people talk over my head. They don't have the patience to speak to me directly, so they talk like I'm not present or as if I were a child or don't understand. It hurts my feelings.

When people talk all at once, it confuses me, and I can't handle it. I have to request that everyone talk one at a time.

Over the years, I've grown quieter and have become a bit of an introvert. There was a period when I felt withdrawn from the family. I felt left out. Micke and the kids sometimes laughed at things I didn't understand, and their computers absorbed them.

At the same time, I don't want too much consideration given to me either. Everyone needs to live their lives without feeling like they need to constantly compensate for me. It's not entirely tragic to fall silent. And there's something about the solitude that I like. I prefer peace and quiet now more than I used to.

There is, of course, sadness about it. A sadness that follows me like a companion who is always present. But I don't always let it in. And sometimes I forget about it and still have great days, like in the past.

We often have a lot of fun together, the whole family. I can't forget that. We've shared tons of laughter. And from laughter, you get strength. I'm so very fortunate. A fantastic family, fantastic job, fantastic home. When I consider what I have, I tell myself not to sit and complain.

CHAPTER 12

Stockholm in December, 2014.

A look at the stage clothes.

———————

"But Marie!"

It's impossible not to let out an excited cry. Marie's stage clothes hang in a large room. Not just a few. And not just any clothes. Leather jacket after leather jacket. It's like looking into a museum of gaud and pop history.

"And check out these pants. You see, there are small mirrors all over the pants. They come from Gucci and cost $5,500 (50000 SEK) twenty years ago. I've never had such expensive stage clothes again. Only Madonna and I have these pants. I used them in London, in Hyde Park. Prince Charles was there, and we said hello to him afterward. He was stiff as hell."

Marie shows me the pants, and it's like we're looking at a work of art. "I love clothes that sparkle and make a statement," she muses. "There should be flare and drama at a concert. Long leather jackets. Short leather jackets. Fun effects."

Marie squeezes between the garments and pulls out a jacket. "Like this matador jacket. It's genuine, the kind they have at the bullfights. We were so big in Spain, and I wanted one for the stage. It was difficult to persuade them. A woman with a matador jacket? Impossible! But in the end, I got one, and we made a few adjustments. It looked so Goddamn cool."

The clothes hang in long rows, one above and one below. A photographer is cataloging them all. Marie doesn't know yet what will happen to them. Sometimes she thinks she should do an exhibition. Or maybe auction them off.

Marie puts on a thunder-blue leather jacket from Helmut Lang. It hangs rather loosely on her. "It's so sad, but I've gone down a size since I got sick. Almost everything's too big."

On a hanger is the yellow dress with large mirror sequins around the neck that Marie wore during the music video for "Anyone." Director Jonas Åkerlund bought it for Marie in a Prada store in London before filming. He liked the color and thought it would look fetching on Marie. The video was recorded in Portugal and began with Marie being taken away seemingly lifeless — in her dress — in an ambulance. Then there's a long montage of Marie wandering around looking melancholic in different settings until she finally walks into the sea. Cut back to the ambulance with an unmoving Marie. Suddenly she opens her eyes and stares into the camera.

Jonas got the idea from an art installation of a man who rowed out to sea and never came back. "Jonas wanted them to put a blanket over me. I thought it would look too scary. I didn't want to appear to be dead," she says. "It was so cold when I went out into the water with the dress."

I touch the dress a bit as my eyes find another garment I recognize. It now hangs glittery and loose, but it's the fantastic bodysuit with shiny, bold colors over a black base that she wore in an early video, "The Big L." She wore black combat boots and looked like a punk version of a circus lion-tamer. She's swinging a long whip while half-naked beefcakes sit in a cage looking frightened — and delighted.

"That video is one of my favorites," says Marie. "It was a Swedish director who did it. His name is Anders Skoog. Jonas and Felix Herngren were assistant directors, Micke Jansson filmed, and Mattias Edwall took stills. I felt so cool in that video. Especially in the tights."

One prestigious and expensive designer garment after another flutters past our eyes. "Oh, this one!" Marie shows me a long silver jacket with a hood covered with sparkling sequins. "It's probably my nicest jacket. It was dazzling onstage. You have no idea. Terribly expensive, but I felt like I had to have it. I was crazy. I spent so much money. Imagine coming from a poor life in a small village in Skåne. It was such a reversal of fortune."

She hangs the jacket back up, pausing to touch it fondly. "Never getting to buy things while growing up has shaped me," Marie continues. "It left its mark, like a hunger that never ends. It was such a change to buy exactly what I wanted. I've never wanted to borrow clothes for various events. I wanted to own what I wore because my fantasy world had come true, and I could finally afford these garments."

We look at the rows of jackets for a while and reach the same conclusion: there is a sense of vindication here.

"It's been so much fun. So unlikely. Once Micke and I were in Milan, in an Armani store, probably about twenty-five years ago. I tried two coats, one cost $2,700 (25000 SEK) and the other $3,000 (27000 SEK). I couldn't decide which one I wanted. Both were stunning. I asked the clerk, who thought I should take the more expensive of the two."

Marie chuckles at the memory. "What the heck, I'll buy both, I thought. You should've seen their faces. It's almost been a compulsion to buy costly clothes. I use them once in a video or interview, and then they just hang here."

Did she ever get any repercussions from shopping?

"No. It fought against the old sadness. It felt good."

The clothes have been a hobby.

"Here at home, I've spent a lot of time at NK and in the shops on Birger Jarlsgatan. Back and forth. Micke and I also used to go to London and go shopping once a year."

Many of the brands among Marie's clothes are ones that I've mostly just seen in photos. Often these are stores that I would never go into, because financially there's no point for me to do so.

"My favorite brands have been Dolce & Gabbana, Prada, and Gucci. Prada has become a bit dull lately," she says. "I also don't like multicolored fabrics, and prefer white, gray, or black. And then a piece of jewelry that stands out."

In the video for "A Thing About You," Marie and Per are impeccably dressed, with Marie in a white shirt, white tie, and black vest. Marie thinks it's a beautiful video but finds it painful to watch, as it was made just before she got sick.

I told Marie that I spoke with Jonas, and he remembered the video shoot and how much fun they had — long lunches, fun and exciting conversations — and how none of them knew what would happen a few days later.

"I know," says Marie. "That was it. That's why I can barely look at those pictures."

CHAPTER 13

Wollongong in Australia.
February 23, 2015.

A big decision.

_____

At the end of January 2015, Marie and Micke traveled to Singapore. They rested up and tried to find a new circadian rhythm a few days before the New Zealand and Australia tour. The tour started at Vector Arena in Auckland. Then concerts followed in Brisbane, Perth, Adelaide, Melbourne, and Yarra Valley, and will end with a few gigs in Sydney and the surrounding area. Four semis transport seven and a half tons of equipment around the continent. Nine Swedes and seven Australians are part of the crew.

I've traveled to Sydney to see Marie in a role we've only talked about at the kitchen table in her Djursholm home, where she meets the audience in large arenas that she has described so many times. The Swedish solo tour was a different affair, with quiet nostalgic nights at various concert halls around the country. Now it will be a different pace, a bigger show. And perhaps even more nostalgic. Roxette will play its treasure trove of songs, but nothing will be from the new album [*Good Karma*] that they've been working on during the fall and winter.

_____

Today we're going to Wollongong, Australia's ninth-largest city with 300,000 residents. It is, like virtually all Australian cities, located by the coast. Large parts of the giant continent are considered impossible to live in, and the whole country has a population of less than half of Italy, approximately.

In Sydney, Marie, Micke, and a recently-arrived Oscar stay at the luxury hotel, The Langham. Per, Åsa, and Gabriel Gessle also stay there, while the band, crew, and I stay at the Four Seasons hotel, a fifteen-minute walk away.

The Langham has a stunning view of Sydney Harbor. Outside is a black van waiting with a driver who will taxi Marie, Micke, Oscar, tour leader Bosse, and me to Wollongong.

A big decision has been made about what's been felt, yet unspoken about during the last few weeks. Marie has decided to sit during her performance. Bosse will help her onto the stage while it's dark and she'll remain seated throughout the show.

During the car journey, Marie says what an enormous relief it feels like. The relief is palpable, and Marie doesn't take it as hard as one might have feared. Now she won't be afraid of falling, nor have to think about balance and moving her feet to avoid cramps. So much anxiety revolves around the foot, and now she can let go of it and concentrate on what she's best at and enjoys doing so much — singing.

"I don't think it's a big deal," she says. "Getting older, it happens to all of us sooner or later — including artists. But you don't have to stop everything just because you have ailments. There aren't many performers my age jumping around anymore, anyway. Now I have to sit, and that's that."

I remind Marie of something Per told me: Bono in U2 also has problems with his foot and leg, and no longer jumps around onstage as he did before.

It takes two hours to drive to Wollongong. Sydney's suburbs give a very civilized impression. We pass orderly homes with tidy gardens. The lawns are as manicured as golf courses.

After agreeing with the decision to sit during the show, Marie says she still misses one thing: having nice shoes onstage. Now she wears sneakers, sturdy shoes that are easy to walk in.

Preferably she walks barefoot as often as possible. "I was barefoot during the Swedish tour. But I don't want to do that anymore. It's often dirty onstage, and it feels a bit gross to stand on it."

Marie continues to wax nostalgic about her shoes. "I love high heels. I dreamed of having them when I was growing up. Later, when I could afford it, during my years with Roxette, I started buying shoes. You have no idea how many shoes I bought. I made up for everything I'd missed. At home, I still have some of the shoes that are so damn good-looking. But I can't comprehend how I walked in them! I loved nice boots. Onstage, I liked high boots when I ran around the most. Well, that was then."

Micke, Marie, and Oscar seem to be in a good and lighthearted mood. They came from a gig at a festival in the Yarra Valley which they describe as purely magical. A tropical velvet night where everything was just right.

Touring life with Roxette started again in 2010 and since then, not only has Marie felt like life has turned around for the better, but the rest of the family also enjoys some return to normalcy. The artist Marie is back, and with her, so is everyday life. And traveling in this way is her everyday life as well — and much more fun. It's the best rehabilitation available. To do what she is best at and what makes her *her*.

That was the turning point, Marie says, as she mentioned before. That Per believed in her. Micke remembers another turning point when he thought everything was changing for the better. Back when Marie was at her sickest, she'd submitted to her suffering, and her ability to assert herself faded, along with her self-esteem.

"But I remember the very moment when I noticed a change," he says. "A few years ago, I criticized Marie for something or said something she didn't like. I don't remember what it was about, but she snapped back at me and called me a fucking idiot. I was so happy — I recognized my wife again!"

———

Suddenly we see the big foamy waves of the Pacific Ocean through the car window. The sun reflects sparkling silver flakes in the ocean.

"Here we are!"

The black van slows down at the city arena. Two young boys are standing and hanging out by the entrance. When they see the car, they grow excited and start shouting and waving. From a distance, they see Bosse helping Marie out of the vehicle. "Wave a little now," says Bosse, and Marie waves to the fans, who shout back, "We love you, Marie."

Backstage we meet Åsa Elmgren, the makeup artist for Marie and Per since 2011. She's also the one who keeps everything flowing behind the curtain. Since nine in the morning, she's been here deciding who will have which dressing room (one for Marie, one for Per, and one for the band), making sure everyone has their wardrobe in place and informing the kitchen about any reqeusts.

Åsa says the organizers think Roxette is straightforward to deal with. Not many lavish demands at all. No diva tendencies. "Is this all?" they usually ask in surprise. Marie wants her room to be warm with no air conditioning, and for it to be neat and clean. There should also be flowers and a way to make a hot ginger drink. There's a faint vanilla scent in the room because Åsa always sets scented candles.

She says they often play arenas where old hockey sweat lingers, and candles mask the odor.

Åsa also makes sure 'Teddy Bear Fredriksson' is on-site, a white and light blue mascot teddy bear. Teddy's a gift from Lasse Bergha- gen [who wrote the popular Swedish children's song "Teddybjörnen Fredriksson" in 1969].

Among the first things Marie does when she comes to the arena is have some dinner. There's always catering available. "On many different levels," Marie says in an insinuating tone. "Sometimes the food is top-notch, but there've been times we went to McDonald's instead." Here in Wollongong, the catering has gone well, as Marie is eating chicken with french fries and seems happy with that.

Inside the dressing room hang a dozen different outfits selected for the current tour. Marie has had the help of stylist Lalle Johnson, except for a chalk-white jacket that Micke found at Zara in Singa- pore. He also went to Prada in Sydney and took pictures of some garments for Marie.

She checks and quickly knows what she likes and what she doesn't. "I want that one, but not those. I can be indecisive when it comes to many things, but not when it comes to clothes. Then I know exactly what I like." They decide that Micke will go to the store when we are back in Sydney and get two black and one white shirt with some bling on the collars.

Marie then flips through what's hanging on the clothes rack. To- day it will be black jeans and a gold shimmering tiger-patterned jacket. "I go completely with my gut on what I want. One day I want a black jacket, the next day white."

Marie is collected and shows no signs of nervousness. "Oh, why would I be nervous? I've been doing this my whole adult life. This is like home to me."

The focus for the evening begins in the makeup chair. This is where Marie prepares herself for the show. She loves to sit in makeup and says that this is due to Åsa. Not only because she's so great at her job, but also because they've become such good friends. Åsa also helps her to relax. "I get completely calm," she says.

"A few times, you've fallen asleep in the makeup chair, Marie," Åsa adds and laughs.

"Yes, but above all, I get in such a good mood," says Marie. "I might come into makeup feeling tired or sad, but I'm on top again by the time we're finished."

Åsa says it can't take too long between makeup and when Marie steps on the stage. They don't want all the energy they've generated while applying creams, eye makeup, and lip gloss to evaporate with impatient sighs and a long wait.

"I never think there's anything wrong with her mood," says Åsa a little later. "She's always positive and has a great fighting spirit. She's so determined. She's a role model to me, and it's admirable that she doesn't give up. If Marie doesn't give up, then who should? On the other hand, she's far too self-critical at times. When she's removing her makeup, she frets over what's gone wrong, even though the audience cheered and thought it was fantastic."

When her makeup is applied, Marie walks around a bit, supported by Bosse, to get the energy in her body flowing. Åsa and I watch them. Bosse looks big and safe next to Marie. He's the one in the touring group who has worked the longest with Marie, ever since the tentative start of her solo career. When Marie and I spoke earlier in the evening, she told me that she'd been difficult with him in the past. She tended to run over everyone and everything. She regrets that she was ever harsh with Bosse because he's the kindest person in the world. And he's dependable, willing to help with anything. Sometimes he even massages her legs to increase blood flow. There's a mutual fondness for one another. "He always says it's gonna be okay and that we'll make it work."

A relatively new member of the gang is Dea Norberg. She sings, dances, and helps to set the mood onstage. "I haven't known her for long, but we quickly became friends. She is so friendly and talented," says Marie.

Marie has learned a lot about preparing her vocals to sing from Dea. Previously, Marie shouted a few times, and then the preparatory singing was done. "Dea knows a lot about this. It's become an important ceremony for us to prep-sing. Christoffer accompanies us, and we sing a few stanzas from, for example, 'The Look' and 'Spending My Time,' songs that require different tones and pitches."

"It's important to cater to my voice so it'll be strong during the evening. The older I get, the more important it is to take care of it. It's crazy how I could crank up the power before. Absolutely insane. I didn't think I had the time or energy to warm up the vocals."

To a certain extent, it's all the years taking their toll, Marie points out. It's no longer possible to be careless. As with everything else, even vocal cords eventually lose elasticity. "Maybe I can't hit as many high notes anymore," she admits. "I prefer to lower the keys. But in a way, I think I sing better today than before. The voice is more fragile, and it has something new and beautiful about it."

The band gathers in the corridor and will soon go onstage. They've been a cohesive group in recent years. Drummer Pelle Alsing and

Clarence Öfwerman on keyboards have been a part of the group from the beginning. Bassist Magnus Börjeson started playing with Roxette in 2010, and Christoffer Lundquist has been the band's guitarist since the latter part of the nineties.

In general, when Marie talks about the band, she gives the same praise again and again about everyone. "We have so much fun. They have a wonderful sense of humor, make me laugh, and are wonderfully supportive." The band members seem like a soft and comfortable wall to lean against.

The band goes up behind the stage, and I see them disappear into the darkness. Åsa follows to powder and with last-minute fixes, and I ask her afterward what she says to them. "You just add a lot of good energy," she says.

Marie goes out first, supported by Bosse. I peek out at them from backstage, at the audience. It's hot and stuffy inside the arena. There are many older fans in the audience — Marie's and my age, however rough that might be to admit. We talk from time to time about the fact that we're the same age. That younger folk don't understand how the years disappear along the way without you noticing how it happened. But you are still the same.

I think about that when I look out at the audience of women with bushy gray hair and bare arms that tremble when they clap along to the first notes of "Sleeping in My Car." Bald men stand with stern arms crossed over their beer bellies. But there are younger people, too. As a band, Roxette turns thirty, and a new generation of audiences has grown up with them. Their parents played Roxette songs while they were growing up. Now maybe the two generations are here together.

Micke and I stand at the mixing table and watch Marie turn into the world-renowned artist she is. She sits barefoot center stage and moves her arms in majestic gestures, looking more confident than when I saw her in Helsingborg and Stockholm on the solo tour.

"Toward the end, everyone in the arena will be standing up," says Micke. I have some doubts, seeing a man sitting broad and stout on a chair in front of me, radiating a soft skepticism. I imagine he was dragged along by the enthusiastic woman dancing next to him. She's spinning her summery dress, her face reflecting a happy reunion of memories that the music evokes.

Get up, I think.

I'm a bit fixated on this gentleman. Roxette never makes him budge. Next to me, a group of women dance to "Dressed for Success" and are having the best time. Åsa, who films the audience as much as she can, smiles at them. Some of her footage will eventually be posted on the blog or Roxette's Facebook page.

More and more people are getting up.

The stiff crowd in Wollongong has softened up considerably, and the hot air is steaming. When Christoffer makes his own Jimi Hendrix version of the Australians' "Waltzing Matilda," the atmosphere is electric.

After playing songs like "The Big L," "Crash! Boom! Bang!," "Fading Like a Flower," and finally, "Joyride," the band leaves the stage. The applause for an encore thunders through the room.

"He'll never get up," I say to Micke, pointing at the grumpy back of the man in front of us.

"He will, I promise."

The evening's last song kicks off, "The Look," and it turns out Micke knows what he's talking about. The man suddenly jumps up with his arms high above his head. I suspect he's swinging his hips too.

Now I don't see a single person sitting anymore.

CHAPTER 14

"It's a miracle that I survived."

Marie's story about the disease.

———

I often think about what a miracle it is that I survived. That I didn't die like so many thought I would.

Since I became ill, a magnetic X-ray of my brain has been done once every third month to look out for any new tumors. After three years, the X-ray sessions were reduced to once every six months. The most acute phase is considered over. It's not a declaration of health, but the odds get better every day I survive.

We did find a shadow of something in my head, and there were different opinions among the doctors about what it was. One thought it was a new tumor, and another said it was radiation injury. The doctors were simply unsure of what they were seeing. And it was the same kind of image, year after year.

Later on, the oncologist who took care of me said that they could either do a more advanced X-ray to look at it or consider it a swelling caused by the radiation. My general condition could decide. And I felt good. I'd managed to stop with the cortisone, and the shadow in my brain hadn't grown. In June 2006, we decided I was healthy. I suffer from damage caused by the radiation, but I'm not sick anymore. It's a swelling, not a tumor, in my brain. It was a great relief to move to this decision. I was so tired of all the examinations. And if we were wrong, we would've known by now.

That summer, Micke told me how close I'd been to death. We talked openly and honestly about everything. Micke told me how he had planned for my passing. And I told him what I'd been thinking but couldn't share. Now we could get close to each other again and be authentic. It was hard to hear these truths, but also quite cathartic. We could begin to mourn what had happened together.

And leave it behind.

It's only recently that I can go to Karolinska Hospital without crying. I hated the hospital environment. The memories were embedded deep within me, and entering the building, even the smell of the building, made everything come back, the memory of the shock, the sadness, the pain. Now those memories have faded.

What helped with my rehabilitation was when Per wanted us to go on tour again. It has undoubtedly been the best medicine. I was thrilled at the prospect of performing again, but also nervous. Would I be able to do it? All the lyrics, would I remember them?

Per has a prompter onstage, but I can't read from one. I have to know the whole repertoire by heart, and it's not easy with my memory issues. But Per jokes with me and claims that I remembered the lyrics just as bad before. In addition, he says all I have to do is aim the microphone toward the audience if I lose track. They know all the lyrics. Oscar has also helped me a lot. He has infinite patience. "Come on, Mom, you can do it!" He's incredibly supportive. He sat and rehearsed the lyrics with me before the Roxette tours.

Per and I decided to start with Night of the Proms. It was the event we were about to do when I got sick. Five songs, just the right amount. The premiere was to take place in Antwerp in front of 15,000 people. We'd perform fifty-three gigs in Belgium, Germany, and Holland.

The premiere was awful. I got the flu and lost my voice. It probably had psychological causes as well, but I simply couldn't sing. We were close to giving up and going home, but the organizer was very determined to keep us. We used playback for the performances, and I mimed through the songs. We used audio files from the rehearsals, where I had sung well, proving it mainly was nervousness wreaking havoc on me. But I also forgot the text and mimed it incorrectly.

Terrible, to say the least — at first. Then Per suggested that we do "It Must Have Been Love" acoustically. Just him and me. At first, I didn't dare, but he persisted. Half an hour before the concert began, I agreed, but only if he promised that no one else knew about it. I wanted to change my mind if I felt like I couldn't do it.

Per told me afterward that the whole band knew. He was sure I could do it, so he told them. And I did! Fifteen minutes later, I thought we should go back to do everything live again. Everything fell in place. After maybe five concerts, everything was back to normal.

I was back.

It was great to meet all of the fans again. Their banners with phrases like "Marie, we love you" and all of the love that they give me.

When Night of the Proms was over, we embarked on a world tour that turned out to be a giant triumph for Roxette. A total of 151 concerts in forty-nine countries.

And now we're on the road again.

During the difficult years, I felt like a constant patient. But to get to stand on a stage again — when the light goes out, and I hear the crowd cheering, it's the most beautiful experience. The feeling today is as wonderful as before. But there's a new element. I feel triumphant that I survived and am still here as an artist.

I can't say enough what it means that Per has always believed in me. He's so positive and supportive. He can lift me into such a good mood, and I then become automatically stronger. I'm always impressed with Per, how he keeps going, writing song after song, believing in Roxette, believing in reaching higher. He makes better and better songs. Thanks to his tenacity, we're back.

———

In the autumn of 2011, we were worried again. In one of the routine X-ray examinations, they saw something they didn't recognize, some activity that might indicate a new tumor. We agreed to a PET scan to be on the safe side. Isotopes, radioactive substances, are injected into the blood. It's a costly and cumbersome procedure with many people involved.

This was done the same day we were to perform in Moscow on our Russia tour. We went straight to the airport afterward. When we arrived at the airport security in Moscow, the alarm went off. There was a big commotion, and the military came running. They thought I was trying to smuggle in something radioactive. That perhaps we had uranium in our luggage. Micke had to tell them it was my blood. That it was I who was still radioactive. I barely made it to the concert on time that evening.

But the good news was that the examination with the magnetic camera showed nothing new. I simply do not have cancer anymore.

CHAPTER 15

Sydney Tower Eye.
February 25, 2015.

An important meeting.

———————————

It's late morning. Marie is resting in her hotel before tonight's outdoor concert in front of Sydney's Opera House. Micke wants to take the opportunity to show Oscar where his parents got engaged. I follow, and we walk to the Sydney Tower in the grayish and rainy yet warm summer-hot city. The streets feel like home, with the same kind of shops and malls here as in Stockholm, Hamburg, or New York. Hugo Boss, Footlocker, Gant, Prada . . .

The Western world's consumer logos are also crowded together here, down under — sneakers from Nike, jerseys from Lacoste, bags from Burberry and Mulberry. Domestic products such as kangaroo leather, fur boots from UGG, jewelry with opals, and knitted garments in possum and merino wool are mixed with the tourist shops. And in the middle of it all — the lookout tower.

We take the elevator to the top. Micke looks around, a bit lost. "It doesn't look the same as twenty-three years ago," he says. At that time, there were smaller tourist shops and not as many guards pointing visitors firmly toward the cashier in the tower, where they're expected to pay to see a 3D film about Australia before gaining access to the lookout point.

We do as they say and put the 3D glasses on, giggling at the mixture of fun and goofiness. We stand and hold a railing during the screening while the 3D film flies us over magnificent Australian views. When the waves rise high on the screen, a mild mist hits our faces.

We're a bit dizzy when we're led into a round room where the full view of Sydney can be seen through large windows in the 309-meter-high tower [just over 1,000 feet]. This is where they got engaged. And the city we're witnessing is the place where Marie and Micke's love story began in December 1991. We walk around and take in the views from all directions, spotting the Opera House and the cricket stadium. Micke talks about Sydney's nightlife back then, in the early nineties, how the fear of HIV left some marks with dark humor. At a bar called Test Tube Factory, for example, waitstaff dressed up as nurses and served drinks from test tubes.

Micke had just ended a long relationship in Sweden and was about to take a long trip. He mainly wanted to go to New Zealand, but his friend Pelle Alsing suggested that Micke stop in Sydney, where Roxette would end a lengthy world tour in front of 11,000 people at Qantas Arena.

And on Sunday, December 15, 1991, on Bondi Beach, the beach outside Sydney, a fragile, tentative connection began between Micke and Marie, which quickly turned into a life-changing event. That evening, about twenty people, some from Roxette and some from an American film crew, gathered to have dinner in town at a restaurant. Marie invited Micke to join, and during dinner, they instantly fell in love.

"I saw myself in her eyes," Micke explains to me as we gaze at the city. "I saw a longing that we shared, loneliness in both of us. Marie was famous, so there was a public perception of who she was. But that persona wasn't the person I saw or felt attracted to, even though I'd always admired Marie as an artist. It's like I knew who she was behind all that. She was missing someone. She was missing me. And I, her. It may sound strange, but that's what it felt like."

Everything moved fast. Only twenty-four hours after Micke started his trip, he met Marie and fell in love. And after the same amount of time with her, he asked if she wanted to get engaged. "At the same time, I was prepared for her to go slow. She was a big artist. How could she be sure that I wasn't someone who wanted to trick her out of her emotions and her assets?" he admits. "In her position, I think it would have been natural to be restrained. But from the first moment, I felt one hundred percent trust from her."

Micke used half his travel money to buy engagement rings, money that should've lasted him for an entire year. The ticket he'd purchased for New Zealand was nonrefundable, so he had to go to the travel agency and cite extenuating circumstances. "I said that I had met the woman of my life and had to stay an extra day to get engaged. The Qantas staff thought it was romantic and cute and helped me. While they were rebooking my ticket, we chatted, and a woman behind the counter asked me about the girl I had met. 'You wouldn't believe me if I told you,' I replied."

"How well did you know each other after twenty-four hours?" I asked.

"Hardly at all," says Micke. "But we knew it was supposed to be us; it was that simple."

Three days after their instant connection on the beach, Micke and Marie were engaged in the tower where we now stand, Micke, Oscar, and I. Micke had casually proposed marriage to Marie in her hotel suite the day before but then formalized it with engagement rings the next day in the tower.

Then off Micke went to continue his journey to New Zealand, while Marie traveled to Stockholm to make her album *The Constant Journey (Den ständiga resan)* with Anders Herrlin. The newly engaged couple had no choice but to get to know each other by talking on the phone.

"That's one of the reasons, I think, why we've remained each other's best friends," says Micke as we take in the views from the tower. "We started by talking to each other. We told each other about our lives and learned early on not to have any secrets from each other. To always be open. It was an ideal way to start a relationship. We got so close through those conversations."

Micke, Oscar, and I glance at the clouds and express common hopes that they will dissipate before tonight's concert. We quietly look over the city and discuss the particular sensation of being so very far from home. Micke says that maybe that feeling made him brave enough to throw himself headfirst into his passion for Marie.

"Had we met in Stockholm or met now, I don't think any of us would have dared to follow our emotions as we did," he muses. "But then, on the other side of the globe, without the internet that keeps us tied to home, it didn't feel as dangerous. We were completely out of our ordinary context. For once, I chose to be spontaneous with my emotions. It's not like me to get carried away like that."

When Micke had traveled to Australia, he sat in tourist class and stopped in Helsinki and Singapore to get the best price on his trip. Life with Marie was something completely different. "After Sydney, we met again in Los Angeles. Marie wanted me to go with her for the rest of the tour," he tells me. "At first, I didn't want to. It felt strange to be some sort of sidekick. But at the same time, I wanted to be with Marie, and the circumstances were what they were."

For Micke, a different life began. Suddenly, he was flying first class, unlike the musicians in the band, who he more identified with. He felt at home with Marie, but band life was familiar. He sums up touring with Marie as fantastic, luxurious, and fun, but sometimes lost and lonely.

"The big reward of going on tour is being able to stand on stage," he says. "The fellowship you feel as a band is so clear, you don't even think about it when you're part of it. But you think about it when you stand on the side. My natural place was with the musicians. I can still feel left out."

The positive still outweighs the bad, of course, says Micke. "What I've experienced is fantastic. Marie was living my big dream, and it was so awesome to experience it with her, with Roxette, with all the fans. To get to live that life. To see her incredible success up close. She invited me to join her in a fantastic and fun life. She made it possible for me, not least financially, to live the life I wanted to live. The ability to sit in a studio and write songs was what I dreamed of. Now I can do it."

Moreover, he got the confidence that comes from experiencing great love. "She gave me self-esteem. I felt grounded with her. She gave me the courage and energy to be who I am because she was who she is. She had everything. She gave me everything. Since Marie became ill, my life has been about taking care of her and helping her. I see it as a kind of universal justice that I got to show her my gratitude for everything she has done for me."

We decide to take the elevator down from the tower. On the way back to the hotel, we'll go into a Prada store to look for the shirts Marie wanted to wear onstage. "I can't believe I dared to do it," says Micke. "I asked her to marry me without thinking about it. The words flew out of my mouth. And I still have it imprinted in my memory. It's crystal clear how Marie is sitting there in her bathrobe in her hotel suite and then standing up with her arms in the air saying, 'YESSS!'"

CHAPTER 16

"We became so powerful together."

In Marie's words.

Did I hesitate when Micke proposed?

No, not for a second! He was the one; I knew it. The one I'd been waiting for. He saw me for who I was. We had a great love, straight away.

It was before Christmas in Sydney. My friend Pähr was there. An extended tour of Asia and Australia had just ended. Pähr had gingerbread cookies and drank mulled wine that we heated in my kettle in the hotel room.

I'd met Micke on a couple of occasions. We'd even had dinner once with our current partners. Since he's also a musician, we had some mutual friends and acquaintances, like Pelle. We casually knew each other but didn't hang out. I thought he was handsome and had always liked him. But one of us was always in a relationship with someone else.

After hanging on the beach that day, I shared a taxi with Micke and Pähr to go back to the hotel. Something was going on even then. But we were shy and cautious. Somewhere along the way, Pähr started complaining that he was hungry and wanted the taxi to stop so he could go and buy a sandwich. Micke and I sat in the car, both a little embarrassed and unsure what to talk about. I told Pähr afterward that it has never taken anybody so long to buy a sandwich!

Later in the evening, the entire Roxette gang went out to eat and celebrate that the tour was over. I asked Micke if he wanted to come along. And that's when sparks started flying. It just hit us. Sparks flying everywhere. Kindred spirits. There he was; there's no better way to explain it. It felt so perfect and right. I knew immediately that Micke was the great love of my life, and all I had to do was let go and follow my heart.

We got engaged, and then I went home to work on my solo album, which I was working on during every spare moment while I traveled. Micke continued his journey and went to New Zealand. The phone bills I received later were probably the highest I've ever seen. Janne Beime, who took care of my finances, called to see what had happened when he saw the bills. He said either the bill was wrong, and there were a few extra zeros in the total, or that love was in the air.

And it was love, of course.

Micke and I started our relationship by talking to each other on the phone. We were on opposite sides of the globe but spoke every day. I've always enjoyed venting and discussing everything between heaven and earth with him. We even did this later when we couldn't be together in person.

The album I worked on after I came home from Australia was *The Constant Journey*. I wrote the lyrics and songs on tour. It's a dark, melancholic album about the loneliness, longing, and vacancy I'd felt in recent years. Anders Herrlin was the producer, and we had such a fun and creative collaboration. He's the best producer I've ever had. He's playful and attentive. We also had the luxury of a larger budget and could choose which musicians we wanted to collaborate with. Anders listened to a lot of atmospheric music back then with emotional and electronic tones, which probably affected me. But otherwise, my feeling was that I was totally in charge for the first time, and that felt important to me. After all the time with Roxette, it was so nice, and I completely needed to express myself in Swedish, on my own terms.

The Constant Journey was composed mainly by me, and I'm proud of it. That album and the single "Sparrow-Eye" are the projects that have meant the most to me because they're so personal and unique. The album's name came from how my life had become a nonstop trek. I was never physically at home, but also, it was my state of mind. I had a hard time feeling at ease, and it's been like that since I was little. I never sat still, and I worried over things. I wrote the songs right before I met Micke. I wasn't feeling great and didn't know where I belonged.

Finding Micke was like finally belonging, like coming home after all those years of searching. And I captured the feeling of finding him in the last song of the album, which is called "At Last (Till sist)":

And then you were just there	*Så var du bara där*
I saw your light in the dark	*Jag såg ditt ljus i mörkret*
Suddenly the sun was shining	*Plötsligt lyste solen*
in the darkness of my heart	*i mitt hjärtas mörker*
Finally	*Till sist*
finally you came	*äntligen du kom*
finally finally	*till sist till sist*
I love you my friend	*Jag älskar dig min vän*
More than you can ever imagine	*Mer än du någonsin tror*
I never thought that love	*Jag trodde aldrig att kärlek*
was a feeling so great	*var en känsla så stor*

Had Micke and I not met, I don't know if I would've continued with Roxette. I couldn't manage the private side of touring; I hung out at bars and drank too much. I was often sad and had a hard time with the press. I always tried to say the right things and felt like I had to be constantly available to everyone with a happy smile. The artist in me grew at the expense of my private life. I had less and less space to be truly myself. And when I found moments to be myself, I was insecure, small, and lost.

With Micke at my side, I regained faith in Roxette and found the desire to continue living that life. Suddenly I could see everything with different eyes.

Life became fun again.

It was vital for us to start an 'everyday life' together when nothing in my life was even remotely close to this. And, everyday life was often something that I missed the most. It was wonderful to stand in the laundry room and iron clothes. Things like that. It was such a nice contrast to my busy life on the road. It didn't feel like it was Marie, the artist, who came back home — but Marie, the person, who finally got to be herself.

A lot was going on with Roxette and me during this time. It took up a lot of space in our life together. Micke handled it well and was seldom bothered by the fact that he often came second, or the hysteria surrounding the band and me. He thought it was fun, like being in an old Beatles movie where the fans chased them. Except this was for real.

And he was so proud of me.

Despite my intentions, we didn't have much home life at all, however. When we got home from a tour, long fax papers curled across the entire hallway floor. It could be from a record company in Indonesia saying we were number one on the charts. Or a record company in Taiwan. I was pampered with success and could hardly imagine life looking any other way.

But when Roxette was number two somewhere, there was eventually a sense of disappointment. We'd wonder if something was wrong. I don't mean to sound arrogant; we were proud and grateful for our remarkable success. But in some strange way, we got used to it, and our expectations for recognition kept growing.

In the early nineties, Per and I experienced massively amped-up notoriety. It caused a commotion just going for lunch somewhere. I ended up unintentionally being the center of attention all the time.

Micke would get irritated at home in Sweden if he booked a table at a restaurant and the maître d' ignored him because he was so focused on me. Or another time, in a carpet store, Micke wanted to look at a rug, but the clerk's attention was solely on me, and Micke was treated like he didn't exist.

When we were newly in love, and out on tour when Roxette was at our high point, Micke was sometimes disappointed that he couldn't go out with me and have a quiet, private dinner. He wanted to do normal stuff occasionally, just the two of us.

But my time on tour was fully booked, especially in the initial years. Socializing was organized and scheduled. There were always different PR people or others who needed time. Plus we couldn't go anywhere without being recognized, and it always became a commotion.

Once in Buenos Aires, Micke booked a table at a restaurant for the two of us within walking distance of the hotel. The only person who knew our plans was the tour leader Dave Edwards. We wanted nothing more than to be left alone, we told Dave. When we entered the restaurant, we realized he'd already told five security guards, who we recognized even though they wore trench coats and slouch hats to hide from us.

We sent them a bottle of champagne.

By the time we'd finished our private dinner, perhaps three hundred people had gathered outside. At that point, we were glad for the guards and happy to get help back to the hotel.

During the *Joyride* tour in Buenos Aires in 1992, Roxette performed in an arena with 55,000 people in the audience. Argentina's largest TV channel showed our concert, and at the same time slot, the competing TV channel showed another Roxette concert from Zurich.

We were everywhere.

It was naive of Micke and me to think we could go out and have dinner like other couples. But we wanted to. As the public tried to get too close, it became increasingly important for us to create more personal space.

When we got married, we wanted to do it with only family, relatives, and our childhood friends. I wanted to get married in tranquility. I pictured a family gathering. We've always enjoyed our respective families. Micke was received with warmth and love by my family. And Micke's mother is one of the most important people in my life.

We wanted to keep the wedding a secret, a private matter, for as long as possible. But it still leaked out. Someone had seen me trying on wedding dresses. Roxette's management spoke with us, telling us that rumors were circulating and warned us against doing something outside of their involvement. This individual said that there would be chaos at the church and that they needed to be involved in managing the event. If we were going to get married, we should go through them. It would help us avoid the chaos and the considerable number of people. It was presented as a well-meant warning.

However, being in charge of the wedding ourselves became a way for us to mark our independence and clarify that our marriage was a private ceremony and not a business event. Many tried to get involved and gave unsolicited advice. But I was so tired of Roxette at this point, and Micke was stressed that our private lives always had to go through management. As if Roxette was getting married and not Micke and me.

We got married in May 1994 in my childhood church in Östra Ljungby and had a party in Mölle. The press found out about it, but nobody caused any trouble. Many fans had also gathered, but it was a happy atmosphere. Everything went well, and we had a fabulous party that lasted for two days.

After the wedding, the same gentleman from Roxette management called us, not to say congratulations, but to tell us how disappointed they were. We were sad that some couldn't be happy for us.

The international press began to speculate whether Roxette would split up. Some of our friends that weren't invited felt excluded and disappointed. I can understand now why Per and Åsa, for example, were hurt. But back then, I didn't see it. The only thing I wanted was for it to be a private ceremony. That's what felt most important.

———————

Six months after we'd met, we were expecting Josefin. She was born in April 1993. We were both over thirty and we loved each other, so why wait?

I'd just become pregnant, and we were having dinner at Per and Åsa's house in Halmstad, planning for the future of Roxette. Recording plans, thoughts on promotions and touring — things that would be developed over the next few years. When I said I was going to be a mother in the spring, the room went completely silent. Then they became excited for us. But it was as if they'd been shocked that we'd have a baby.

When Josefin was a few months old, we went to Capri to record the album *Crash! Boom! Bang!*. From there, we went on a world tour, and Micke, Josefin, and a nanny came with us. I wanted to be with them, but I had to work.

The whole family lived in my apartment on Västmannagatan. The nanny moved into Micke's apartment in Södermalm. But we longed for a home to share that was ours.

On Capri, faxes often arrived with various housing proposals. The house we were currently renting in Djursholm was one of those proposals. We immediately agreed that this should become our new home. We could also build a studio for ourselves, something we often wished for.

Many wondered what would happen to Roxette now that there were children. But it worked out fine with Josefin, and then came Oscar, and after that, Per and Åsa had their son Gabriel. None of us minded touring with children, so we simply took our families with us.

Just before Micke and I met, I'd bought a summer place in Haverdal. It's located outside Halmstad on the west coast with beautiful natural surroundings and a sandy, four-kilometer-long beach. The house in Haverdal became the first home that Micke and I created together. But we seldom had time to be there, and when we were, it was hard to find time alone. Fans came from all over the world and would sneak around in the bushes. One Midsummer [the Swedish holiday], when we'd finished eating out on the terrace, we had to duck and slowly walk back inside with our dinner plates so as not to be seen. But we were soon discovered. *Excuse me, but I've come all the way from Antwerp,* they'd say. What could we do? I gave in and signed their autographs.

Eventually, we sold that house.

We also longed for warmer temperatures. We fantasized about buying a house in Spain, but it didn't happen until I became ill. Micke has since told me that he agreed to Spain not only because of the warmer weather, but also because he wanted me to feel like I was realizing one of my big dreams before I passed away.

The house in Spain may not have been the world's best deal, as the real estate market has looked since the financial crisis, but emotionally, it was right.

When we were in Spain, we did our best not to let the disease consume us. Doctors, hospitals, and anxiety were absent. We even surveyed the schools in the area and thought that we might move there permanently. But we eventually realized that we couldn't take the children from the security they had with their friends at home in Sweden. Everything was already too uncertain around us. In Sweden, we were also only ten minutes away from Karolinska Hospital with all my doctors. My medical records were there. In the end, it felt safer to stay in Sweden.

Micke and I have never had a separate group of friends. We spend most of our time with each other. When Micke and I are out on the town, we enjoy getting some food and then checking out a local band. We like going to the jazz club Fasching. Or having a night out on the town at other clubs. When the children spend the night at grandma's, we sometimes host parties at home.

My friend Marika reminded me of that the other day, how we've said that if there's one thing we want to be remembered for, it's our parties. We loved hosting festivities for our friends. Often the planning was at least as much fun as arranging the kind of event that we'd want to attend ourselves. We spent a lot of energy, time, and money on food, drink, and entertainment. We tried to find the right chef, the right guest list, and the best available bands. One rule we had, though, was there was no assigned table seating. We have too many memories of ending up stuck next to some boring guy we had to talk to. We only invited fun people and served the best food and drinks we could find for our guests, who could choose where they wanted to sit or stand or who they wanted to talk to. The best reward was when friends got in touch afterward, telling us that they had as much fun as we did.

Now our life together has changed. It's taken quite some time to find our way back. I don't know how to describe it. But it wasn't until I became ill that I learned how to allow myself to feel some of the downsides of life. In the past, it was full throttle all the time. In that way, I feel more like myself today. We've been forced into new conditions, both good and not so good.

Micke has been by my side all along. He could've easily asked for a divorce. I would've understood. I've been utterly dependent on his support during this time. But for him, the idea of leaving me has never existed, even though I realize that he has had a hard time with my illness. He usually says that he wouldn't have been able to stand himself if he'd walked out on me. That he chose for better or worse with me. We'd shared ten years of 'better.' It's as simple — and complex — as that.

We've always been able to help each other. When one is weak, the other assumes a solid and supportive role.

We wanted to continue living a fun life, even though I got sick. We wanted to show the children that life could still be joyful. But there's still underlying grief, which makes parenting difficult. I've been seriously ill and sad for most of their upbringing. Micke was filled with despair and still feels guilty that he may not have been there enough for them.

Time doesn't heal all wounds. We learn to live with the wounds instead. It took Micke and me eight or nine years of illness and rehabilitation before we started mending and progressing together again. And today we were strengthened by getting through this.

CHAPTER 17

Sydney Opera House.
February 25, 2015.

An evening filled with honor.

—————

There's a majestic, almost ceremonial mood in the air. Roxette plays by the stairs leading up to Sydney Opera House. What an iconic building. To perform here is to win a world tour trophy of sorts.

"It's a great honor and definitely one of the highlights of the tour," Per writes on the Roxette blog.

While Marie is in makeup, I take a walk around the building. Thick marble-like clouds have been gathering in the sky all afternoon. The leftover afternoon heat adds a heaviness to the evening. The cloud cover paints the sky an impermeable black and hides that the moon looks different here.

Sydney's second most famous building, Harbor Bridge, is illuminated and sparkles across the water. The high arches of the giant bridge have given it the nickname "The Coathanger," but I think it's more reminiscent of an amusement park attraction. During the day, a stream of people crosses the five-hundred-meter-long bridge, so high up that they look like ants walking on a branch.

The darkness has also deepened over the botanical garden located close by. From time to time, I hear loud parrot cries from the trees and other mysterious sounds, perhaps bats. Much of Australia feels like England, but not when it comes to flora and fauna. A fist-sized spider was found in one of the tour buses, and some panic broke out, until an Australian identified it and told us it wasn't toxic. It can bite, admittedly. But it's no worse than a good pinch.

Outside the Opera House, by the water, a sign says "Seal Resting Area" and lists some rules on handling any seals and sea lions that may appear. The advice is to keep a respectful distance. Sea lions are faster than one would think, and they can, like spiders, bite if they feel cornered.

The arch-shaped stage echoes the same aesthetic as the Opera House itself. The audience seems younger than the one in Wollongong and is more city-dressed. Marie sits on her tall chair and looks mischievous as she sweeps her eyes over the audience. A triumphant smile lurks in the corners of her mouth.

So I'm back, bet you didn't think that, she seems to be thinking.

Marie wears a black jacket, a black shawl with white skulls, and black jeans with fringed holes over the knees. Her feet are bare, and her toenails are painted black. She rests one hand on the microphone stand and looks more like a queen than ever. Dea has on heels high enough for both her and Marie. Christoffer is wearing a glittery shirt and a black hat pulled over his long hair that the sea wind grabs at. Pelle is in a faded shirt with an American West Coast look. Clarence has on a tasteful gray-blue suit and gray hat, Magnus is entirely in black with vest and wide trousers, and Per wears a gold brocade jacket.

The band members look unusually good tonight. Roxette enters the stage, and two large black-and-white image projections play. The whole scene looks very stylish and artistic.

Per sums it up — "[Isn't this] the most beautiful setting ever?" Bassist Magnus wants to capture the moment by taking a selfie with Per in the middle of the ongoing concert, with the Opera House and the audience in the background. A moment to save and show at home. But unfortunately, the picture only shows two faces and darkness.

The audience is more readily excited here than at the last concert. The show turns into one big love fest when the crowd sings along with the acoustic version of "It Must Have Been Love." An American in his forties looks at the backstage pass around my neck and keeps bugging me, saying, "I came from New York to see Marie. Please, make sure I get to take a selfie with her later. Please. Think of how far I've traveled to see her." I look into his pleading eyes and start to soften. He presents his case to Micke, who's not as easily convinced. Nothing comes of it.

And when I see Marie after the concert, I can clearly understand his concern for his wife. Marie has collapsed on a chair with a beer in her hand and is so tired that her eyelids occasionally close in the balmy night.

Her smile is soft and faint when I tell her how nice I thought she looked during the concert and how great she sounded. But at this point, she can't give any more. She isn't able to meet and talk with fans or take photos with anyone.

Soon, we pack up in the black van that drives us back to the hotel. By the gate to the restricted area, Per steps out to sign autographs for a large group of fans who've gathered.

"I can't do it," says Marie. "It's not possible, no matter how much I would've liked to do so. This evening wore me down."

Oscar waves to some fans, who eagerly wave back. A few days later, it will be on the Roxette blog. *Thank you for waving back, Marie! You've made my day!*

The Australian head of Live Nation hosts a party at The Langham, the hotel where Marie and Per are staying with their families.

They offer the band food and drink, but Marie is determined to go to bed. Not even a single glass of champagne to celebrate how nice the evening turned out interests her. "No, I'm going upstairs. The best thing after an evening like this is to be left alone. It's because of my injury. I can't handle a lot of commotion around me. That's the way it is these days. Sadly, I can't keep up in the same way as before. We used to have a lot of fun together during the tours, going out for dinner or hanging out at the bar. I'd like to go to the party, but I need to go to bed."

The rest of Roxette is used to Marie wanting to rest in the room during her free time. They celebrate the concert while Marie takes some personal time. At a table, the children of the Roxette members sit together: Gabriel Gessle, Nikki Öfwerman, Emma Alsing Skoog, Ingrid Lundquist, and Oscar Bolyos. Micke says that it warms his heart when he sees them like that, like a giant family get-together.

"Sometimes I felt like Roxette competed with our private lives," he tells me. "That it intruded on our family life. But today, it feels the other way around, like Roxette is an extended family. They grew up with the other members' children and have a close relationship with them. Our kids love Roxette so much, the tours, the songs, the people.

"Roxette has done so much good for us that I feel emotional when I talk about it. We get an electric charge from touring with Roxette. When you feel the power of the audience, it's purely magical. Marie and I met thanks to Roxette, so the band is central to us. I feel deep gratitude for what the group has contributed to our lives."

At the party, I sit at the same table as Per, Åsa and two Australian execs from Live Nation. Per seems upbeat and happy that everything went so well. Two gigs are left, then the tour breaks until mid-May. Then Europe awaits; the tenth of May is the premiere in Milan.

"It's remarkable that Marie has managed to come back," says Per. "But I'm not surprised. She has such a winning mentality. She's one of the few who can mentally cope with a journey like this."

He tells me about the evening when he and Clarence saw Marie perform for the first time after she became ill. "It was at the concert event called Stjärnklart, where several different artists performed. Marie sang a few songs. It was obvious to me then that she had her amazing strength back. The power she had before she became ill was there. Her voice was strong enough to convince me that she'd be able to come back. And I know she lives for this. And what would she do otherwise, sit in Djursholm and drink expensive wine? The only thing she really wants to do is sing and play and interact with the audience."

———

The next day I walk to Marie's hotel. The night before was late and generous with drinks and champagne, and now I'm also tired. *The Daily Mail* has a jubilant review praising yesterday's concert, and the headline is about how Marie is still an unbeatable style icon with her short platinum blond hair: *She's STILL Got the Look*. Otherwise, the reviewers describe a nostalgic evening, and even if Marie doesn't always reach the high notes she managed before, she makes up for it with feeling, presence, and a fighting spirit.

Marie opens the door herself when I knock and seems perky and in a good mood. She's not wearing makeup, the black nails are gone, and she looks comfortable in a relaxed training jacket. The leg is so-so, but it is what it is. In any case, she's slept well and says she enjoyed the solitude.

"Before, loneliness was the worst thing I knew, but now I love it," she tells me. "Like last night [after the show in the hotel room], I can relax and it doesn't even matter if I trip. I just get up again. Nobody needs to worry. I'm calm and relaxed. I brush my teeth and journal what I've been thinking about, like planning for the future and what I want to do. For example, I'd like to go home and start painting and drawing again."

I ask if she's sad when she doesn't hang out with the gang in the evenings. She says she's not. "I'm sad that my foot is acting up. But you know, I feel more secure now," she explains. "I've learned to see everything from a brighter perspective. For so many years, I wallowed in darkness. But I chose not to give up. For every tour that goes well, I become more and more convinced. I will fight and fight until I can't do it anymore."

I am struck by how often Marie returns to words like struggle, fighting, and not giving up. Where does the drive come from? What makes her push herself?

She thinks about it for a moment. "From my childhood. Life was difficult, but I learned how to take care of myself. I always pushed ahead and asserted myself. The same with singing. I fought to progress with it. To get into the music department at folk school. To get a record contract. The anxiety pushed me forward. Now I'm at peace with myself, but that iron will remains the same."

CHAPTER 18

Qantas Arena in Sydney.
February 27, 2015.

A story in itself.

———

Before tonight's concert, I have dinner backstage at the arena with Marie. She chooses salmon, which she usually likes, but not quite in the style that it is cooked here. She's delighted about the apple pie for dessert, which I have to help her eat. One hand twists much like her foot. It's hard for her to spoon up the cake. She's straight-forward and unapologetic when she asks for help.

"That's my injury," she says. "It's the hand — do you see how it twists?" She holds up one hand and shows me. "I get so damn tired of it, that I have such little power."

Micke comes in with his computer. He shows Marie a picture that makes her burst into a big smile. It's Josefin and the cat Sessan posing in the melting snow back home in the garden. The seasons are changing, and the first flowers of spring are emerging. "Oh, we'll be going home soon!" she gushes. "How I long to see Jossi and the flowers!"

The conversation seems to give an extra energy boost to Åsa in the makeup area.

———

The evening at Qantas Arena has a magical charge. People dance and sing along, and the atmosphere is joyful. The fans in the large arena seem to know every song, "Sleeping in My Car," "Joyride,"

"Dangerous." But when Dea sits down at the piano and starts playing Marie's fine-tuned melody "Watercolors in the Rain," the audience falls silent. The piano and Marie's voice resound through the room.

Seems I've been running
All my life
All my life
Like watercolors in the rain

The chorus in "Watercolors in the Rain" reminds me of our conversation in her hotel room the night before. I know she's extra happy to sing it because she wrote the music herself, and Per added the perfect lyrics; words that convey who she is. When I hear her sing the lines about how she's been pushing ahead through life, I'm close to tears.

And it strikes me when I see her singing in her brilliant white jacket that, in addition to being a fantastic singer, she's also come to embody a story. Not just the story of survival but also of fragility and vulnerability. This is what happened to her, and it can happen to anyone. You do not have to hide because of it. You can share your destiny and pain with others.

The whole arena is in sync with Marie. She extends her arms, taking in the love that emanates from the audience. The crowd wants to share her story. And I think that their generosity toward Marie is deserved since she so graciously shows the people in the audience how much they matter.

I think that these enthusiastic fans can feel this.

This is a good night.

Micke watches Marie from the side of the stage. Like the audience, he's full of emotion. "I feel so proud when I see her. Proud in a completely different way than before. Marie gives so many people hope. People are often having a hard time, even more difficult than we can imagine."

But now, touring life is over for the time being. In two days, it's time to fly back to Sweden again. "I'm relieved that we're going home now," says Micke a little later. "Even though touring life is fun, I'm always worried that Marie won't have the strength and that something might happen to her. It's a great relief every time a tour is over and has gone well. But then, when we get home, we long for the road again. The concern exists at home as well."

The anxiety characterizes Micke's life — and the grief he tries to contain. He describes the difficulty of keeping an emotional life alive with sadness at its core. He has to switch off sometimes, but this comes with a price. You risk becoming a switched off person in general. "Every day, I try to come to terms with our fate, but it is difficult," he explains. "Life is not like mathematics where plus and minus cancel each other. The joys do not neutralize the sorrows; they live next to each other."

Micke describes a few strategies he uses to deal with the difficulties. One has been routines — everyday life with the children, which can feel comforting when everything else has been fear and chaos.

The second strategy has been about learning to live in the moment. "When I felt that the anxiety was eating me up from within, I stopped looking ahead," he says. "Anxiety is always associated with the future. I trained myself to live in the now to keep my anxiety at bay. In the present, it's too late to worry."

And the present is what it is.

"The joy of having experienced the great love surpasses the sadness that Marie became ill," he continues. "It's tragic that we were so young when it happened. Marie was forty-four years old, and I was forty-five. But the happiness we experienced before that, nothing can take it away from us. I'm so grateful for our children and the relationship we have. With Marie's radiation injury, the situation as it is now is the everyday life we live in. Today I have lived longer with Marie after the illness than before."

After the concert, the participants gather as usual in the band's dressing room. Oscar has poured champagne for everyone; it has become his special duty during the tour. Marie joins for this part, and they recap the evening. What went well and what didn't work. Everyone is pumped and euphoric and needs to chat about it, even though there might have been an accident or two.

"Christoffer and Per may have injured their fingers. They sometimes strike the strings so that their fingertips bleed," says Marie.

I'm struck by how Marie is perhaps the most central figure on tour. Above all, she's the one in the spotlight. But she's also the one who often ends up on the outside, a little to herself. All eyes are on her onstage. But offstage, she's a bit in the shadows.

"I think everyone who has some type of disability understands what it's like," says Marie when we discuss it. "If you find it difficult to walk, difficult to read or manage in another way, you'll be left out. It comes automatically."

But it isn't just her injury, she points out. "The music industry is a men's industry. It's hard to be heard sometimes. It drives me crazy when men address each other and talk over my head."

"Marie is the hub of Roxette," says Christoffer. "She's the one giving Roxette wings." He agrees that in the very masculine and business-oriented music industry, she's not given the respect she deserves.

"She's connected to her emotions. She's open and easily moved. That's what her art is based on. It's what the audience feels and wants, what they're affected by," says Christoffer. "At the same time, some people think a person with her fragility doesn't quite belong up there. Some might regard her as weak or easy to overlook. But her sensitivity is a positive trait, and Roxette's success is based on it. I can't think of anything more important than listening and being supportive of her."

And being seen as more delicate, Christoffer sadly points out, also partially has to do with the fact that she's a woman. Christoffer noticed how people have talked over Marie even before she became ill, as with many other women in the music industry.

"I've produced a little over a hundred records with musicians and artists worldwide, and I've seen the pattern of speaking around female artists and musicians," Christoffer says. "My experience is that men often come to the creative process with a finished plan in mind that they want to realize. Nothing wrong with that. But when the unexpected happens, interesting results can occur. And a large number of men can get uncomfortable with this. They think they're losing control and want to keep to the plan. Their plan. On the other hand, many women have a remarkable ability to capture what's happening in the moment without caring about what it's called, what genre it belongs to, or what the outside world thinks."

This ability to capture the moment is why Christoffer prefers to work with women. "Men taught me in my early years, and since then, I've completely retrained with teachers that are almost exclusively female artists. My music has improved and become more original.

"It's because it's always men who have the power. It's always about control and power. The power over the computer, the tape recorder, the instruments, the recording process, the money, the schedule, the release. All of this has been pushed to the limit in the organization around Roxette. Probably because it's so big and successful, and there's so much money involved.

"I think some men in the organization feel a subliminal frustration, maybe even anger, over being dependent on Marie. Sometimes it's almost as if she's perceived as a problem. It was the same before she became ill. A crazy culture if you ask me. Really crazy, actually."

Christoffer shakes his head. "Men generally seem to be afraid of what cannot be measured, controlled, or planned. Afraid of their feelings. And actually, afraid of women. It may sound extreme, but that's my experience."

"I don't need to comment on that further. Christoffer says it so well. That's also

how I think it is," says Marie.

CHAPTER 19

Djursholm in May, 2015.

Time for silence.

In Marie's words.

You know, Helena, I think we should end the book here. It's spring, and I love spring, and I love that I'm home again. It smells like hagberry trees from my garden. The lilacs are coming soon.

The blackbird sings. I recognize the sound well. Even though I've forgotten how many other birds sound, I always remember the blackbird's song.

The nightingale is probably the bird I like best. It comes in the middle of May and is my favorite sign of spring. I wait for it every year. Once, when everything was at its worst, a nightingale flew up and sat right by my window. It came right to me as if with a message. Exactly what I needed at the time.

Birds are a personal passion of mine. I love to listen and try to figure out what kind of bird I hear. When I was seventeen, my then-boyfriend Stefan and I were out with a group of bird-watchers, and I learned to recognize many species. Before I got sick, I knew most. Sometimes the memory comes back, like an "a-ha" moment, and other times I draw a complete blank. It hurts to lose such knowledge.

Ever since I was little, I've taken refuge in nature. It's my favorite place in the world. Flowers. I adore flowers, how they bloom, how they smell, how beautiful they are. I can look at a bouquet for any length of time. They're enchanting. White roses! Outstanding, aren't they? They're gorgeous. Before my illness, I knew what many kinds of roses were called. Now I don't remember any names.

We've had lovely roses in the garden, all with pretty names. One night the frost came, and several roses died. We also had a giant hagberry tree that got infested and dropped all its leaves and flower clusters. Stuff like that makes me sad. But one spring, the hagberry tree came back to life again. What a joy!

Death and life. Life and death. Nature comes with both pain and joy. It is the story of everything.

In our garden, there's a mighty and ancient linden tree. It must be over a hundred years old. I love being close to the linden; it gives me strength. Trees grow so slowly and patiently. They provide such strength. Following the seasons through trees is a gift. I live for things like that. I'll take a linden tree over Facebook any day, for fuck's sake!

Stress destroys the brain. This stress that people live with today, with their cellphones and computers. No one talks to each other anymore. *Let's sit and talk to get a proper connection,* is what I want to tell people. Is anyone able to do that anymore? To give each other that? Listen and talk, for real.

Per spends a lot of time in the digital world, which means our connection gets worse and worse. He lives in his bubble. We used to reach each other much better, with more laughter and more heartfelt conversation. For our type of relationship, we need to take the time. Nobody does that nowadays. Everyone is completely engrossed in their computers.

Everyone except for me. That's how it feels, at least.

Earlier, when Oscar, Josefin, and Micke were busy with their computers, I sat somewhere else and cried because I couldn't keep up. I'm not criticizing them; they live in the world as it looks today. But I felt hopelessly left out. That's what happens when you're not on top of everything digitally. Now I'm used to it and don't feel as left out anymore.

Well, sometimes.

Oh no, now I'm gonna cry.

Marie, do not cry now! I have to rebuke myself sometimes.

I'm grateful that I'm alive, even though I cry. I have a wonderful home. I can surround myself with beauty. My home is my castle, where I can breathe, where I can play the piano. When I'm home, I walk around and putter. I enjoy taking care of myself and not being as afraid of falling. I know exactly how to move, and I'm not ashamed if I faceplant. It's still the hardest thing for me to have everybody watching me and risk falling.

Unfortunately, my twisted foot has made it harder to handle the pedal while playing the piano. It's important to continue writing songs. I always memorize them and stopped using sheet music a long time ago. Sitting with paper and pen, waiting to see what happens, it's exciting — both drawing and writing.

Sometimes I write a word on a piece of paper. A word that means a lot to me. Such as *tranquility*. I wrote it down the other day. Tranquility is the most beautiful word I know. Peace and quiet. That's how I live now. There was a hell of a lot of action in my life before. An insanely high pace. It's nice to get older and see life differently.

Keep tranquility close to your heart.

Tranquility is a beautiful word that sums up the calmness of everything.

But now I want to show you something . . .

Marie goes and picks up a gray notebook. She sits down and leans over it so no one can look inside. This is where she keeps her most secret lines. Those that take much time to get down but are so vital to her. She writes with a pencil, a few lines on each page.

Marie reads aloud a line: Inez in silence.

This is either the beginning or the title of a song that I hope to finish someday. It will be called "Inez in the Quiet" and will be about my mother. She was always quiet and lived on the sidelines. Dad took up so much space. The rest of us sang and were up to a lot. Mother was the kindest person in the world as she toiled with her tedious job at the factory. And it didn't get easier for her with her illness. She had to fight hard to make ends meet. She was an amazing person. I want to finish this song one day. She meant so much to me. I want to break her silence with this song and finally give her a voice.

Everything became challenging the day I became ill. I no longer cope well with stress. Going out to perform is stressful but a great joy — a luxury. But I take it easy. Not too many gigs in a week. I'm resting properly between events. I sleep at least half an hour in the middle of the day. I do what I can to find my inner peace and deal with one thing at a time.

I'm afraid of moving around outside on my own. It's tragic. I don't even go out into the garden by myself anymore. I need someone to hold on to, even short distances. In the spring, if it's warm outside, I like to go out and sit for a while and enjoy the sun. I like the warmth so much.

The long Swedish winters are quite difficult. I get cold easily. This winter we celebrated Christmas at home in Sweden. I never want to do that again. Christmas trees — not my thing. And I really dislike the darkness. Next year I want the warmer weather again. I'll look forward to our Spanish house. It may not be more than fifteen degrees Celsius (fifty-nine degrees Fahrenheit) during Christmas in Spain, but at least it's bright out.

Time is short. We only have one life, so why sit around in the darkness?

I've survived. I've learned that the rug can be pulled from under you at any time. Anything can happen. But life also contains miracles. Like, who would've thought I'd be on a stage again?

Okay, I don't really stand anymore.

I sit there.

But I sing and meet the audience. A miracle!

It's awful that my foot started acting up. As if there's no end to this mess. Something new pops up all the time. And that's the way it is. The hardship will never end. It's not possible to live without pain.

Still.

Fragments of happiness also show up and sparkle like diamonds in the rough.

I've learned to enjoy the little things. A streak of sun. The first blossom. Even a really good sandwich.

It finally feels like I have come to terms with the fact that I have a radiation injury to live with. That's how it turned out. I lost many years to the disease. And there's sorrow in getting older. But every day, I think of how thankful I am to be sitting here.

And that I can still sing.

That's what I know. The only thing I'm good at.

Well, one more thing. Keeping the kitchen tidy — haha!

When I made my album *The Constant Journey*, there was a song called "Time for Silence (Tid för tystnad)."

It's not much I ask for	*Det är inte så mycket jag begär*
The few moments when you're here	*De få stunder när du är här*
When we learn to live	*När vi lär oss leva*
We see each other so rarely	*Vi ses så sällan är nästan*
are almost always apart	*alltid isär*
and feel who we are	*och känna oss som vi är*
We have had to start over	*Vi har fått börja om*
so many times over	*så många gånger om igen*
again	*om igen*
If only we had time for silence	*Om vi bara får tid för tystnad*
When we see and hear and listen	*När vi ser och hör och lyssnar*
Give us time for silence	*Ge oss tid för tystnad*
When our togetherness listens	*När vår samhörighet lyssnar*
We have chosen a life to live in	*Vi har valt ett liv att leva i*
which costs courage and all our energy	*som kostar mod och all vår energi*
But I think there is a place for us	*Men jag tror det finns en plats för oss*
and to get there	*och för att komma dit*
time must carry us	*måste tiden bära oss*

That's exactly how I feel today. I must have time for silence.

There must be time in life for silence.

Damn, there's so much stress out there. Everybody's running around and getting worked up. Sometimes I think about what a relief it is not having to participate. Even though I'm sort of trapped in a cage. I've been forced to remove some elements from my life. Like shopping. I can no longer shop. Now, before a tour, a stylist brings clothes to my house. I find other ways. It's nice to have gotten away from what occupied my time before. The disease is a tragedy, but it brought good things with it. I learned to sift, sort, and value the good from the bad.

What's essential in life? It sure as hell isn't shopping at NK!

Life is more than stressing over nonsense. I say no to a lot these days, to everything that feels like a hassle. There are days when I feel powerful from what I've been through. I recognize what's important. What to care about and how to let go of silly shallowness.

Thirteen years of my life have been marked by sadness. But I never gave up, even when I've been grief-stricken. I've remained connected to the creative part of myself.

Painting, composing, singing.

I sit and write a few lines. Work on what a line should look like. Then I delete it and start again, trying to find the right letters. I keep doing this until I am satisfied. The line should be beautiful, and it should say something. It usually takes a long time to get to it right.

Other people may take it for granted that they can write eloquently and understand what they've written. But for me, the greatest happiness on earth is when I get my words down on a piece of paper the way I intended.

Expressing ourselves in the ways we can is so much more important than anything else.

That and maintaining a love for life, regardless of what might happen. Regardless of what becomes our destiny.

EPILOGUE I

It's the height of Swedish summer. The rain pours down. We are in the building that makes up Marie's dressing room outside the Maritime History Museum. It's not enough to say the rain is pitter-pattering against the roof. It's more like thundering down. Almost 13,000 people wait patiently under umbrellas and rain ponchos in the museum's large garden outside.

Marie is concerned. "All those poor people in the audience. How will it go? They're gonna get completely soaked."

And how will it go for her and the band? Even though there's a roof over the outdoor stage, the wind is so strong that the rain will be whipped up anyway. Makeup artist Åsa Elmgren comforts us. It will be fine. Rain also sets the mood — a kind of brave togetherness.

Otherwise, fatigue characterizes the mood of the band. Possibly it's the stuffy air in the building. Or it's that we're approaching the end of Roxette's thirty-year celebration tour. The tour started in Russia in November 2014 and has now completed fifty-seven concerts out of the sixty-two planned in Europe. After tonight, only four gigs are left, in Rättvik, the Faroe Islands, Finland, and finally Norway. But after New Year's, they'll start again. In January 2016, the tour continues in South Africa and in April, South America.

———

When Christoffer and Dea join Marie in vocal warm-ups, Marie and Christoffer talk about the group's fatigue. *What's the matter with us? Have we ever been this tired?* There's nothing to do but dig deeper. Marie turns to Dea, and they start to warm up their voices. At first, they sound as if they are riding a roller coaster:

sch . . . jaja . . . hey hey . . . hoy hoj . . . hooray! . . . nana . . . lala . . .

And eventually comes: *What's the time . . .?*

Marie sings the introduction to "Spending My Time."

"Deep breaths," says Dea when Marie finds it challenging to reach all the way up.

And Marie takes deep breaths. For the song and the performance. A car pulls up to drive her, Per, and Bosse through the rain to the stage entrance. Before they get in the car, Per tells Marie that "now we will rock Stockholm's ass."

They smile at each other under the umbrellas.

The concert goes just as Åsa predicted. It's raining so hard that everyone kind of gives in to the downpours. Someone from the crew jumps onstage and shovels the water away between songs. Per's smile is broad, and Christoffer stomps defiantly in the rain so it splashes around his legs.

Marie's voice overpowers the sound of the rain:

> *Hold on tight, you know she's a little bit dangerous*
> *She's got what it takes to make ends meet*
> *The eyes of a lover that hit like heat*
> *You know she's a little bit dangerous . . .*

When I hear Marie sing "Dangerous," I think of what she told me earlier. When she struggled to talk and find the words after the last brain operation, the melody to "Dangerous" was the first thing that came to mind. She hummed the melody repeatedly, and eventually, the words came back.

Music and song have always been a source of strength and comfort for Marie. When other ways of expression failed her, the music was still there. It built a bridge to the words, and the words turned into singing. Whatever we discussed, the joy and sorrow of childhood, the successes, the loneliness, the struggle and the desire to recover from the illness, singing has been the hand she held in life.

She will never let go of it.

EPILOGUE II

There will be no more tours with Roxette. Their performance in South Africa in February 2016 was their last, even though they had fourteen shows booked in Europe later in the summer.

Unfortunately, Marie fell and hit her head in April 2016. What exactly caused the incident isn't apparent, but one thing is clear: she can no longer cope with the pressure and stress of touring life. She finds it even harder to walk. Her foot twists and cramps and she must have help with the slightest movements.

Marie:

It's a great sorrow to realize that my time with Roxette is over. We're such a damn good band. I think the record we just released [*Good Karma*] is one of the best we've recorded. Our time together is one of the best things that has happened in my life. We had so much fun. I got to know so many people around the world. Roxette's started as an unlikely success, same with the idea that I could even become a star. I've been through it all, and no one can take that away from me.

At the same time, it's a relief for it to be over. I realize that the pressure has been too intense in recent years. Stress must be removed from my life, quite simply. I should've stopped touring earlier. But I wanted at all costs to keep my identity, who I feel I am. And I'm thankful that I got to experience again what Per and I have done together for years. To have wonderful fans all over the world. To meet them and receive so much love from them.

I'm deeply grateful for that.

I want to be as genuine and sincere as possible with this book. It's terrible for the family and me that it's happened the way it has. Thankfully, I find it easy to cry, and crying relieves grief. When pain is unresolved, it's hard to feel any joy.

Despite everything, I still have my happiness and, above all, my fighting spirit! I will never give up and will fight to maintain my ability for joy and creativity as long as I can.

My time and energy right now will go primarily to train myself to walk again. I just tried out a splint that stretches the foot and supports the leg. When I went to check it out, they wondered what kind of splint I wanted. "Give me a rock 'n' roll splint," I said jokingly. But they took me in order. I get to have a splint in black leather!

New lyrics still come to me, and these lyrics carry a feeling that is important for me to follow; they help me to remember what is good and well. All the love I feel for Micke, for the family, and for life.

I still love to sit in my garden. To get a little moment in the sun. I feel a spark of strength, and with that, I can continue to be creative and do what I like.

I will not get stuck in the dark. I'll fight for what is bright and beautiful every single one of my remaining days.

Marie passed away on December 9, 2019
in the aftermath of her illness.

AFTERWORD

"**A** collection of poems. Maybe we could make one of those?"

We'd finished the memoir, and Marie Fredriksson had lots of ideas for what to do next. Despite deteriorating health, her desire to create was as strong as ever.

"Sure," I said. "A beautiful book, small and thin, but comforting."

"So many beautiful words," Marie sighed. "I want to capture them. I want everyone to read them."

Marie was a fighter. I've thought and said it many times, and I'll continue to do so. She showed remarkable resilience in managing the physical struggles of a terrible disease and grew to understand the mental fortitude needed for psychological survival. Marie was determined to remain herself; vibrant, complicated, utterly human. To soak up life right up to the very end. Marie never wavered in her quest to commune with the world. She wanted to share her moments of transcendence and offer consolation to those full of doubt.

The light, despite everything.

In Sweden, Marie Fredriksson is equally famous as a solo artist as she is for being in Roxette. The songs she's recorded, written, and collaborated on are considered national treasures, often played at weddings, funerals, baptisms — any occasion worth calling upon a feeling of life's grandeur. She is the embodiment of big feelings and bottomless emotions — piercing our hearts without ever coming across as disingenuous or sentimental.

It's not an easy task, sincerity. Many traps line the path. Many artists take the notion of love and the longing for love and use it to elevate themselves. They seem to say with a flirty wink that everything beautiful and powerful comes from them. Some artists may want to express those big and bottomless emotions with sincerity but can't resist adding a bit of sarcasm. They fear pretension, so take the magical elements of love and longing and reduce them to a joke. Still others treat big emotions as so sacred they can only be viewed behind dust-free display cases or appreciated in gloomy chapels. They seem to want to keep spirituality free from the mundanity of life.

Or you're a new artist finding your voice. You want to convey emotions, know the words to use and have a rough comprehension of their meaning, but you lack depth. You simply aren't able to translate those big feelings and bottomless emotions yet, and you might not ever improve.

Marie Fredriksson avoided such traps. She took the big words, the foggy concepts, the search for love and longing, the actual scent of love, and *told a story*. Her words, even when they were words written by or for someone else, never fell flat, shallow, or silly. They were — and are, for ages to come — truly sincere, like one heart speaking to another, her heart to ours.

Find a Marie song and play it; listen to her now, and picture her in her house by the sea. Hear how beautiful it is.

Her lyrics are like the words she wanted to put in a collection of poems but never had the chance. Even if we can't read her book of poetry, we have these beautiful words from one of her most well-loved songs to enjoy with unabashed sincerity.

"There's Still a Scent of Love (Ännu doftar kärlek)":

For there's still a scent of love	*För ännu doftar kärlek*
and hope turns into faith	*och hoppet blir till tro*
The winds are still blowing	*Ännu blåser vindar*
but settles into peace	*som stillar sej till ro*
I always want to give you time	*Jag vill alltid ge dej tid*
to accept my longing	*att ta emot min längtan*
And I hope that you will do the same	*Och jag hoppas du tar vid*
if my faith grows weak	*när min tro är svag*

I often think of Marie, the strong woman at the kitchen table who never let anything keep her down. I think of her stubbornness, a trait that could be quite difficult to deal with at times. Marie wouldn't budge. If she wanted something done a certain way, then that was it. She also had a rather cheeky sense of humor, and we spent much time giggling and laughing together. I want those qualities on record because it was important to Marie that she never come across as 'too sweet' or 'fancy.'

People often get in touch with me, wanting to discuss the book. To tell me how much her words and thoughts have meant to them. They talk about her as if she was a friend.

Marie would have loved that.

Helena von Zweigbergk
Fall 2022

DISCOGRAPHY

TEMPORARY COLLABORATIONS

ALBUMS

MaMas Barn — *Barn som barn* — 1982

SINGLES

Strul — "Ki-i-ai-oo" — 1981
MaMas Barn — "Mammas barn" — 1982

MARIE FREDRIKSSON (SOLO)

ALBUMS

Het vind — 1984
Den sjunde vågen — 1985
... Efter stormen — 1987
Den ständiga resan — 1992
I en tid som vår — 1996
The Change — 2004
Min bäste vän — 2006
Nu! – 2013

COMPILATION ALBUMS

Äntligen (Marie Fredrikssons bästa [1984–2000]) — 2000
Äntligen (Sommarturné) — 2000
Kärlekens guld — 2002
Tid för tystnad (Marie Fredrikssons ballader) — 2007

LIVE ALBUM

Äntligen Live! — 2003

COLLABORATIVE ALBUMS

Den flygande holländaren — 1988
A Family Affair — 2007

SINGLES

"Ännu doftar kärlek" — 1984
"Het vind" — 1984
"Den bästa dagen" — 1985
"Silver i din hand" — 1986
"Efter stormen" — 1987
"Sparvöga" — 1989
"Så länge det lyser mittemot" — 1992
"Mellan sommar och höst" — 1993
"Tro" — 1996
"I en tid som vår" — 1996
"Ber bara en gång" — 1997
"Äntligen" — 2000
"Det som var nu" (with Patrik Isaksson) — 2000
"2:nd Chance" — 2004
"All About You" — 2004
"A Table in the Sun" — 2005
"Sommaräng" — 2006
"Ingen kommer undan politiken"
(Complainte pour Ste. Catherine) — 2006
"Där du andas" — 2008
"Where Your Love Lives"
(English language version of "Där du andas") — 2008

"Kom vila hos mig" — 2013
"Sista sommarens vals" — 2013
"Det är nu!" — 2014
"Alone Again" (with Magnus Lindgren and Max Schultz) — 2017
"I Want to Go" — 2017
"Sing Me a Song" — 2018
"Sea of Love" — 2020
"Stay" — 2021

ROXETTE

ALBUMS

Pearls of Passion — 1986
Look Sharp! — 1988
Joyride — 1991
Tourism — 1992
Crash! Boom! Bang! — 1994
Have a Nice Day — 1999
Room Service — 2001
Charm School — 2011
Travelling — 2012
Good Karma — 2016

REMIX ALBUMS

Dance Passion: The Remix Album — 1987
ROX RMX Vol. 1 (Remixes from the Roxette Vaults) — 2022
ROX RMX Vol. 2 (Remixes from the Roxette Vaults) — 2022
ROX RMX Vol. 3 (Remixes from the Roxette Vaults) — 2022

COMPILATION ALBUMS

Rarities — 1995
Don't Bore Us — Get to the Chorus! (Roxette's Greatest Hits) — 1995
Baladas en Español — 1996
The Ballad Hits — 2002
The Pop Hits — 2003
A Collection of Roxette Hits (Their 20 Greatest Songs!) — 2006
The Rox Box / Roxette 86–06 — 2006
XXX — The 30 Biggest Hits — 2014
The RoxBox! (A Collection of Roxette's Greatest Songs) — 2015
Bag of Trix (Music from the Roxette Vaults) — 2020

LIVE ALBUM

Live: Travelling the World — 2013

SINGLES

"Neverending Love" — 1986
"Goodbye to You" — 1986
"Soul Deep" — 1987
"I Want You" (with Ratata and Eva Dahlgren) — 1987
"It Must Have Been Love
(Christmas for the Broken Hearted)" — 1987
"I Call Your Name" — 1988
"Dressed for Success" — 1988
"Listen to Your Heart" — 1988
"Chances" — 1988
"The Look" — 1989
"Dangerous" — 1989
"It Must Have Been Love" — 1990
"Joyride" — 1991

"Fading Like a Flower (Every Time You Leave)" — 1991
"The Big L." — 1991
"Spending My Time" — 1991
"Church of Your Heart" — 1992
"How Do You Do!" — 1992
"Queen of Rain" — 1992
"Fingertips '93" — 1993
"Almost Unreal" — 1993
"Sleeping in My Car" — 1994
"Crash! Boom! Bang!" — 1994
"Fireworks" — 1994
"Run to You" — 1994
"Vulnerable" — 1995
"You Don't Understand Me" — 1995
"The Look ('95 remix)" — 1995
"June Afternoon" — 1996
"She Doesn't Live Here Anymore" — 1996
"Un Día Sin Ti" — 1996
"No Sé Si Es Amor" — 1997
"Wish I Could Fly" — 1999
"Anyone" — 1999
"Stars" — 1999
"Salvation" — 1999
"The Centre of the Heart" — 2001
"Real Sugar" — 2001
"Milk and Toast and Honey" — 2001
"A Thing About You" — 2002
"Opportunity Nox" — 2003
"One Wish" — 2006
"Reveal" — 2007

"She's Got Nothing On (But the Radio)" — 2011
"Speak to Me" — 2011
"Way Out" — 2011
"It's Possible" — 2012
"The Sweet Hello, The Sad Goodbye (Bassflow Remake)" — 2012
"The Look (2015 Remake)" — 2015
"It Just Happens" — 2016
"Some Other Summer" — 2016
"Why Don't You Bring Me Flowers?" — 2016
"Help! (Abbey Road Sessions November 1995)" — 2020
"Let Your Heart Dance with Me" — 2020
"Tú No Me Comprendes" — 2020
"Piece of Cake" — 2020
"Fading Like a Flower" (with Galantis) — 2022

MARIE'S PLAYLIST

Below is a list of songs that were significant in my life. —
Marie

"I'm A Believer" / The Monkees
I watched the TV series when I was a kid. I liked drummer Micky Dolenz so much.

"Valleri" / The Monkees
The very first single that I bought for myself.

"Nights in White Satin" / The Moody Blues
Tina and I both cried when we first heard it. We thought it was the most beautiful song that we had ever heard.

"Everything I Own" / Bread
Another song that Tina and I cried about because it was so beautiful.

"To Love Somebody" / Bee Gees
So nice to listen to their vocals. This one makes me so happy.

"No Milk Today" / Herman's Hermits
Another favorite for Tina and I. We loved it immediately!

"I Never Loved a Man (The Way I Love You)" / Aretha Franklin
Few songs hit me so deeply. I have sung it to myself on so many times, and have also sung it live. Very significant.

"Revolution" / The Beatles
"Helter Skelter" / The Beatles
"I Want You (She's So Heavy)" / The Beatles
I completely lost my mind after watching the Beatles on television for the first time. They sang "She Loves You" and I could not have been many years old at the time. The three songs that I selected

above show their slightly more raw side, which I loved. I was especially a fan of George Harrison.

"Paint It Black" / The Rolling Stones

I listened to the Rolling Stones at the same time as the Beatles, and liked them just as much. It was as if the bands expressed two different sides of me, one calmer and the other more aggressive. I felt at home with the Rolling Stones' tough style.

"Lookin' Out My Back Door" / Creedence Clearwater Revival

I love John Fogerty's voice. Creedence has so many great songs that it's really hard to choose just one.

"You Really Got Me" / The Kinks

What an amazing song! Not so long ago, I met Ray Davies. Actually, he tried calling out to me, but I did not see him because of my visual impairment until it was too late. So sad!

"Pinball Wizard" / The Who

This song really stood out for me. I liked their hard rock mod style, but didn't challenge myself to try something similar. It was only later that I was a bit more daring.

"Get Up (I Feel Like Being a) Sex Machine" / James Brown

I thought that I was going to combust when I first heard this one. I was twelve years old and went to a disco for the first time in my life, in Klippan. I had never heard anything like this single. It just suited my soul and I was beaming.

"Purple Haze" / Jimi Hendrix

Jimi was so important when I was growing up. I loved his music, his attitude and his clothes. He was a role model, a complete icon to me. I was so terribly sad when he died.

"Här kommer natten" / Pugh Rogefeldt

Pugh has meant an incredible amount to me. I first saw him in concert when he played Halmstad. Then he shaved his head and

I thought he looked so cool. I loved that look. Subsequently we have sung together a few times.

"Guldgruva" / Pugh Rogefeldt

I covered this song on my album *Min bäste vän* in 2006.

"Din bäste vän" / John Holm

This is my favorite song by John Holm, and I covered it on *Min bäste vän*. I also sang on John Holm's 1988 album *Verklighetens afton*, which meant a lot to me. John writes fantastic lyrics.

"Tin Soldier" / The Small Faces

The wonderful song that Per Gessle and I met over. We both thought that it was the best song we had ever heard.

"Blue" / Joni Mitchell

Joni has always been a great source of inspiration for me, and this is probably my favorite song of hers. I also love the way that she handles the guitar. Her strings are often tuned in a chord, creating "open tuning" and giving her a mellow, moody sound.

"Big Yellow Taxi" / Joni Mitchell

And this is my second favorite song from Joni Mitchell. She's one of two artists that shaped me the most, Jimi Hendrix being the other. Two extremes, like the Gemini I am!

"Dream a Little Dream of Me" / The Mamas & the Papas

Mama Cass simply had a wonderful way of singing.

"As Time Goes By" / Billie Holiday
"Strange Fruit" / Billie Holiday

When I was young, I listened to a lot of jazz. I bought a lot of old singles, including Billie Holiday among others. I have listened to her so much.

"All of Me" / Ella Fitzgerald

She was incredible at improvising. I learned this song by heart.

"Blackberry Way" / The Move
A fantastic song. So beautiful!

"Get It On" / T. Rex
I loved everything that T. Rex did, but this is my favorite.

"Everyday" / Slade
This was the first ballad I heard from Slade. Noddy Holder's vocals on this one are wonderful.

"All the Young Dudes" / Mott the Hoople
Ian Hunter has such a special voice. I also thought he was so cool with his black glasses.

"I'm Not in Love" / 10cc
I first heard it on Radio Luxembourg and flipped out.

"You've Got a Friend" / Carole King
Incredibly beautiful lyrics and a very special voice.

"Without You" / Harry Nilsson
What a voice!

"Dreamer" / Supertramp
I met my first love Stefan at a Supertramp show.

"Owner of a Lonely Heart" / Yes
I have always liked Yes and bought many of their records. A lot of their music was instrumental and experimental, but of course this was one of their big hits.

"Mr. Blue Sky" / ELO
I have so many memories of this song. ELO sounded so fresh and new when they arrived, and they arranged their songs so uniquely.

"All I Wanna Do" / Sheryl Crow
The lyrics are great on this one. I really like Sheryl.

"Stone Me Into the Groove" / Atomic Swing

I absolutely loved this song when it came out. Niclas Frisk sings it so fantastically well. I would really like to sing with him at some point.

"I Don't Know What It Is" / Rufus Wainwright

A very good friend introduced me to Rufus Wainwright's music. I immediately thought that he was so heavenly good. Sadly, my friend died when he was younger than I am now. I have a hard time listening to this song now, but this is a great track.

"Nocturne in E Flat Major" / Chopin

I love listening to classical piano music.

I have collected these songs on Spotify in the playlist "Kärleken till livet" (attached to the user "piratförlaget").

Here is also a URL and QR code:
https://tinyurl.com/MariesPlaylist

ILLUSTRATION CREDITS

Images are courtesy of Marie Fredriksson's family.

Additional images provided by Mattias Edwall (cover, page 215, author photo), the ARChive of Contemporary Music, and the collections of Jason Buck, Matthew Chojnacki, Ivan Kelava, and Oliver Zimmermann.

The following specific illustrations are courtesy of Alamy photography agency:

Pages 8, 9, 228, 229 (TT News Agency/Alamy Stock Photo)
Color plates — pages 8, 25/top (dpa picture alliance/Alamy Stock Photo)
Color plates — page 13/top (INTERFOTO/Alamy Stock Photo)
Color plates — pages 13/bottom, 23/top, 23/bottom left, 24 (TT News Agency/Alamy Stock Photo)
Color plates — pages 25/center, 26, 27 (WENN Rights Ltd/Alamy Stock Photo)
Color plates — page 25/bottom (ZUMA Press, Inc./Alamy Stock Photo)

ABOUT THE AUTHORS

Marie Fredriksson was a Swedish singer, songwriter, pianist and painter, who was best known internationally as lead vocalist of pop rock duo Roxette, which she formed with Per Gessle in 1986. Roxette achieved global success with albums such as *Look Sharp!* and *Joyride*, and had multiple hits on the *Billboard* Hot 100 including four number ones — the most for any Swedish act. Select singles include "The Look," "Listen to Your Heart," "Dangerous," "It Must Have Been Love" (from the film *Pretty Woman*), and "Joyride." She lived with her family in Sweden, where she passed away in 2019.

Helena von Zweigbergk is one of Sweden's most respected authors, and is also a journalist, radio host, and film critic. Novels include *Run for Your Life* (2006), *Out of the Mouth of the Volcano* (2008), *Things You Just Say* (2009), and *The Heart Beats On* (2013).

Here is me as a child. There are only a few photos of me this young. The family photo includes everyone except for my brother Sven-Arne, who is behind the camera. Here also is a familiar memory of my dad in his mail car. The color photo includes the red shoes that were mine as a child. They were hand-me-downs and a little worn, but they made me feel wonderful, and of course I ran around a lot in them since I couldn't sit still.

O ur family home in Östra Ljungby. Every home in Östra Ljungby looked the same. However, notice the roses that mother was so meticulous with. Plus a few photos of my mother and father. Mom worked so hard taking care of us all.

My friends from folk high school in Svalöv would come to visit and hang out. Stefan (my first real boyfriend) is the guy in the red shirt, and then there's an additional shot of him and I at his parent's house trying out different instruments. The black-and-white photograph is from a Christmas production, when I was still deciding between theater and music.

KI-I-AI-OO
STRUL IGEN

A few more early photos of me singing, before releasing my first physical recordings. In 1981 I released a 7-inch vinyl single with the band Strul, and then a full-length album with Mamas Barn in 1982.

S ome of my different early looks! This includes the infamous dress from 1984 by Ika Nord (see the black-and-white photo). It had one sleeve, so my aunt thought it was obviously unfinished. Plus my brief stint with red hair, and an attempt at floral patterns.

The red hair continued at the start of Roxette's first LP *Pearls of Passion* in 1986. The album never attracted too much attention abroad, but was a big hit in Sweden. Per and I tried many looks during this period as well, but I finally landed on a short blonde hairstyle that stuck with me over the years.

Efva Attling (*top left*) became one of my best friends when I moved to Stockholm, and also gave me my first pair of leather pants. The photo of the two guys is Anders Herrlin (*blue shirt*) and Clarence Öfwerman (*red shirt*), who were both important in helping to develop Roxette's sound; Clarence was a producer on every Roxette album since the beginning. Per and I held the same dream of making it in the US, and here are two early Roxette shots from the US, including an image of us snacking on a promo tour. I was so proud of that hat!

Roxette in Dortmund, Germany (November, 1989).

Touring the world in support of the *Look Sharp!* album. On stage, walking the streets (notice the little girl in the background — wonder what she's thinking?), plus some typical tourist shots in Washington, DC (White House) and Australia (Sydney Opera House).

The gentleman with me (*bottom left*) is Rolf Nygren from EMI, who came up with the idea that Per and I should become a pop duo. This lead to Roxette's first single, "Neverending Love." Here also are a few awards photos; the gold ones are Rockbjörnen ["Rock Bear"] Swedish music prizes, and the plaques are Grammis [Swedish Grammys] from 1989.

Here's me with Elton John (*top left*), the Bee Gees (*bottom right*), and Tina Turner (plus Ronald McDonald for their CEMA promotion that we both participated in) — Tina later invited us to her fantastic home for dinner.

Plus also a *Joyride* gold award presentation (*bottom left*) from EMI Germany, with my sisters Ulla-Britt and Tina as surprise attendees.

T he photo of me in the yellow dress is from the music video for Roxette's "Anyone," directed by Jonas Åkerlund in Portugal. The other two photographs are from the music video shoot for "You Don't Understand Me," a fantastic song by Per and Desmond Child (Bon Jovi, Joan Jett, Cher); the video was directed by Greg Masuak in black and white, and featured a traveling theater company.

R oxette in 1995 during the *Crash! Boom! Bang!* days.

The bottom photograph was from my first public outing since my diagnosis. It's from 2003 when Per and I received achievement medals from King Carl XVI Gustaf of Sweden "for appreciated achievements in Sweden and internationally." Since I had lost my hair at the time from radiation, Marie Dimberg and I shopped for this leopard print hat just prior to the ceremony.

A sample of solo releases, including the albums *Hot Wind* (*Het vind* / 1984), *The Seventh Wave* (*Den sjunde vågen* / 1986), *In a Time Like Ours* (*I en tid som vår* / 1996), the hits compilation *Finally* (*Äntligen* / 2000), and the single "Sparrow-Eye" ("Sparvöga" / 1989).

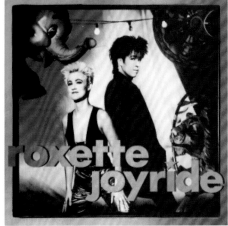

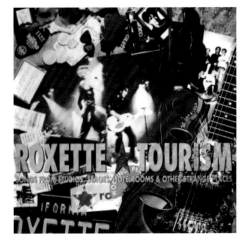

In the US, Roxette had its biggest album sales with *Look Sharp!* (1988), *Joyride* (1991), and *Tourism* (1992) — a "tour album" consisting of new studio recordings plus live tracks. While both *Look Sharp!* and *Joyride* sold over a million units in the US, they each shifted an additional 9–10 million copies in the rest of the world.

Despite a difficult distribution situation in the US, Roxette's popularity continued to flourish in the rest of the world after *Joyride*. This included the successful albums *Crash! Boom! Bang!* (1994), *Have a Nice Day* (1999), and Roxette's final release, *Good Karma* (2016), among others.

Roxette's first single "Neverending Love" from 1986, which initially used a hand-drawn cover instead of a photograph.

"The Look" (1989) became Roxette's first worldwide hit and reached #1 in the US. It was only the third US #1 for a Swedish act, following Blue Swede's "Hooked on a Feeling" (1974) and ABBA's "Dancing Queen" (1976).

"Listen to Your Heart" repeated at #1 in the US, and "Dangerous" peaked at #2.

"It Must Have Been Love," buoyed also by the success of the Julia Roberts film *Pretty Woman* (1990), also hit #1 in the US, as did the "Joyride" single (not shown) in '91.

However, similar to Roxette's albums, physical single distribution (plus radio airplay) became a difficult situation in the US.

"The Big L." didn't receive a US release, for example. Roxette's last single to hit the *Billboard* Hot 100 was "Sleeping in My Car" in 1994. However, Roxette continued to release successful singles in the rest of the world, with more than 25 additional releases.

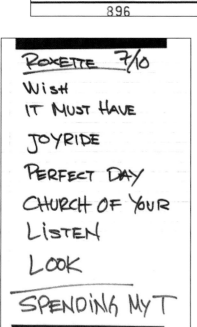

F an tickets from the tours to support *Look Sharp!* and *Joyride*. The short hand-written setlist was from Sky Church at Experience Music Project [now MoPOP] in Seattle, Washington. Only 200 fans were admitted to this intimate performance on October 7, 2000. Plus a New York City ticket from the Beacon Theatre in 2012.

Due to the large amount of cortisone I was taking as part of my treatment, my face swelled up so much that I was unrecognizable. I really didn't want to show my face at the time, so when the cover art was due for my album *The Change* (2004), Micke suggested that I draw a self-portrait. This piece was titled *Lonely*, and captured how I looked at the time . . . at least on the inside.

From my solo tour of Sweden in 2014, with Micke in the wings on piano.

P romotional tour posters pasted up in various cities. Included is a stop on March 16, 2011 in Riga, Latvia to support the *Charm School* LP; a solo appearance to promote *Nu!* in Malmö, Sweden on March 7, 2014; plus a Roxette *30th Anniversary Tour* date in Stuttgart, Germany on July 2, 2015.

That's me with makeup artist Åsa Elmgren (*bottom photos*). Plus a backstage toast from Roxette's tour of South America in April, 2012.

R oxette's staging during the inauguration of Friends Arena in Stockholm, Sweden on October 27, 2012. Attendance was 46,000, along with a television audience of 1.7 million. Other performers on the bill included Sweden's The Hives and First Aid Kit.

Stage shots from what became known as *The Neverending World Tour*, stretching from 2009 to 2016. The top photo was from Munich, Germany (December, 2009), center was from Perth, Australia (February, 2012), and the bottom image was taken in Toronto, Canada (August, 2012).

More stage shots from *The Neverending World Tour*. Top and center photos were from Perth, Australia (February, 2012), and the bottom image was from Amsterdam, Netherlands (May, 2015).

From a sold out show at Heineken Music Hall in Amsterdam (May, 2015).

My daughter Josefin took this photograph of Per and I thanking the crowd in San Francisco, California (September, 2012).

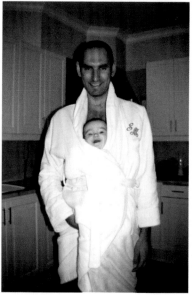

S ome early family photos. After touring I really enjoyed getting back home, relaxing with Micke and the kids, and doing some typical chores. Here is also a photo of the kids having fun at the grand piano (*top right*). I had always dreamed of owning one, and it was one of the first items that I bought when I started earning money.

A few more recent photos. Me with Micke, the kids, and Micke's mother (*top right*). Plus a photo with my beloved magnolias (*top left*). Flowers, trees, birds, and nature have always meant a lot to me. Such peace and quiet here in my garden.

T wo family portraits by photographer Mattias Edwall. Micke, me, Josefin, and Oscar, plus Micke's mother Berit in the bottom photo.